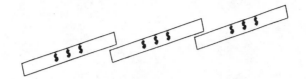

Reaching the Full Cost of Quality in Early Childhood Programs

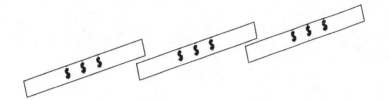

Barbara Willer, Editor

A 1990–91 NAEYC Comprehensive Membership Benefit

National Association for the Education of Yc

1834 Connecticut Avenue, N.W

Washington, D.C. 20009-5786

National Association for the Education of Young Children
1834 Connecticut Avenue, N.W.
Washington, DC 20009-5786

The National Association for the Education of Young Children attempts through its publication program to provide a forum for discussion of major issues and ideas in the field. We hope to provoke thought and promote professional growth. Except where specifically noted as an official position of the Association, the views expressed or implied are not necessarily those of the Association.

ISBN: 0-935989-42-0

NAEYC #137

Cover and interior design: Barbara Willer

Printed in the United States of America

Table of Contents

ABOUT THE AUTHORS

SUE BREDEKAMP is the Director of Professional Development for NAEYC. She is editor of NAEYC's *Accreditation Criteria and Procedures of the National Academy of Early Childhood Programs, Developmentally Appropriate Practice in Early Childhood Programs Serving Children Birth through Age 8,* and *Guidelines for Appropriate Curriculum Content and Assessment in Programs Serving Children 3 through 8 Years of Age.*

MARY L. CULKIN is Co-Principal Investigator of the Child Care and Education Project at the Colorado University at Denver. She is a preschool director for the Friends British Primary School in Boulder. Her expertise is focused in early childhood educational administration, including planning, practice, and training. She has extensive experience in interdisciplinary projects; her current work bridges early childhood education and economics.

ELLEN GALINSKY served as NAEYC President from 1988 to 1990. She is Co-President of the Families and Work Institute in New York City. A noted authority on early childhood education, her work has been instrumental in shaping the emerging field of work and family issues. She is a prolific author, with publications directed to parents, researchers, the business community, as well as the early childhood field. Her work is widely respected in each of these different arenas.

SUZANNE W. HELBURN is Professor of Economics at the University of Colorado at Denver. She is noted for her expertise in the economics of child care and the economics of poverty, particularly related to low-income families headed by mothers. Another area of interest is social studies curriculum development and teacher training.

JOAN LOMBARDI is an Early Childhood and Public Policy Specialist from Alexandria, Virginia. She currently serves as a member of the NAEYC Governing Board (1987–1991) and is the 1990–91 chair of NAEYC's Public Policy Committee. For the past 2 years, she served as chair of NAEYC's Advisory Panel on Quality, Compensation, and Affordability. She is a co-author of the NAEYC publication, *Speaking Out: Early Childhood Advocacy.*

JOHN R. MORRIS is Professor of Economics at the University of Colorado at Denver. He is particularly interested in applied economics, especially the economics of poverty and the economics of child care.

BARBARA WILLER is the Public Affairs Director of NAEYC, working extensively on public policy and media issues. As primary staff liaison for NAEYC's Advisory Panel on Quality, Compensation, and Affordability, she compiled the *Quality, Compensation, and Affordability Action Kit,* and authored, along with Lynn C. Johnson, *The Crisis is Real: Demographics on the Problems of Recruiting and Retaining Early Childhood Staff.*

Introduction

Barbara Willer

THE FULL COST OF QUALITY is the concept underlying a public education campaign by the National Association for the Education of Young Children (NAEYC). As the professional association for the early childhood field, NAEYC has strived to improve practice in the field for more than 60 years. NAEYC has also worked to improve public understanding and support for high quality programs for young children and their families. The Full Cost of Quality campaign continues that tradition with one important difference. The campaign not only promotes better public understanding of what constitutes quality in early childhood services, it also stresses that if any quality component is missing, then quality for children is compromised. The full cost of quality therefore holds a dual meaning. It refers to the costs of program provision while fully meeting professional recommendations for high quality, while also implying the social costs that are incurred when quality is lacking.

This book is designed as a handbook for early childhood professionals and others interested in improving the quality of early childhood services available to young children and their families. It is a resource of information and tools to build a compelling case for improving the quality of existing early childhood services and to take action to bring additional resources into the early childhood system.

New resources, both public and private, are beginning to be seen. In late 1990, Congress created a new federal child care program and significantly expanded the Head Start program. The task now is to carefully plan how new resources will be utilized. The materials in this volume will help advocates and policy makers focus on the long-range goal of assuring quality services for all children in the planning process. While new resources are coming, they remain limited. For example, new federal funding is primarily limited to low to moderate income families, while child care costs stretch family budgets at what appear to be comfortable levels.

This volume is divided into three sections. The first section provides background information, defining the underlying factors which have led to the Full Cost campaign and stressing the need for immediate action. Chapter 1 presents an overview of the issues and introduces the key concepts of the campaign. In Chapter 2, Mary Culkin, Suzanne Helburn, and John Morris provide an economic perspective to explain the lack of affordable, quality early childhood care and education that so many families face. Ellen Galinsky outlines the research literature related to the elements of quality and suggests the costs of not providing quality for children, their families, and their teacher-caregivers in Chapter 3.

The second section presents the NAEYC professional recommendations for quality which are relevant to the Full Cost of Quality campaign. These include criteria for high quality in early childhood programs (Chapter 4) and guidelines for compensation of early childhood professionals (Chapter 5).

The volume's third section is designed for taking action. Chapter 6 is specifically tailored to individual programs, in centers, schools, and family child care homes. It presents a framework and data for estimating the full cost of quality. National estimates and projections are suggested, and specific information is provided for estimating the full cost of quality in an individual program. These estimates may also be aggregated to estimate the full costs of quality program provision in a particular community, region, or state.

While change at the program level is essential, widespread improvement in program quality will require broad community support and action. Chapter 6, written by Joan Lombardi, is a guide for organizing a community coalition to address issues related to the full cost of quality. Specific activities are suggested for coalitions to assist programs to reach full quality. Finally, a list of resource organizations and materials is presented for additional sources of information.

This book is meant to be a working tool! The information presented here is designed to lay a broad foundation of community support and action. We envision this book and the efforts it hopefully generates as "priming the pump" for additional activities to help all sectors of our nation recognize that we can't afford to shortchange America's future: the full cost of quality must be paid in early childhood programs.

DEFINITIONS

Traditionally, child care and education have been viewed as separate and distinct services. NAEYC believes that for young children care and education are integrally related; the younger the child, the more impossible it is to make any distinctions between the two. For very young children, all learning is embedded within a caregiving function, whether provided by parent or another individual. Even as children mature and education becomes more distinct from care, caregiving remains important.

Good programs for young children serve both care and education functions. Throughout this volume, **early childhood program** is used as the preferred term for referring to any program providing services for young children. When necessary in the context of tradition, "child care" is used to refer to programs which children attend while their parents are employed or otherwise unavailable. It should be remembered, however, that the basic components which define high quality in a program chosen to provide a good "educational" experience to a young child are the very same qualities needed to provide a high quality experience for children while their parents are employed.

Early childhood programs include any part- or full-day group program in a center, school, home, or other facility, that serves children from birth through age 8. This definition includes child care centers, private and public preschools, family child care, kindergartens, and the primary grades of elementary schools.

Teacher-caregiver is used to stress the fact that individuals who work with young children—whether in a center, family child care home, school, or other setting—provide both care *and* education. The term "staff" should be interpreted to include a family child care provider, even when that individual is self-employed and is the only adult engaged in the provision of care and education in the setting.

ACKNOWLEDGMENTS

This volume reflects the efforts and input of a number of individuals. Of particular note has been the work of the NAEYC Advisory Panel on Quality, Compensation and Affordability. The Panel's efforts in 1989 and 1990 focused on defining the "Full Cost of Quality" concept and developing recommendations for NAEYC action in this area. Panel members have been particularly helpful at every stage of this book's development, from conceptualization to final review. Panel members during this time included Rebeca Barrera, Jerlean Daniel, Ellen Galinsky, Robert C. Granger, Janice E. Hale, Joan Lombardi, Kathy Modigliani, Jim Morin, and Marcy Whitebook. Appreciation is also extended to Nancy H. Brown, David Gleason, Lana Hostetler, Paula Jorde-Bloom, and Sharon Lynn Kagan for their thoughtful reviews and suggestions. The editor also expresses great appreciation to the authors whose contributions made this volume a reality: Sue Bredekamp, Mary L. Culkin, Ellen Galinsky, Suzanne W. Helburn, Joan Lombardi, and John R. Morris.

The Full Cost of Quality Must be Paid

Barbara Willer

HIGH QUALITY early childhood programs provide a warm and nurturing learning environment for young children. Adults who work with children in high quality programs understand how young children grow and learn and know how to provide the materials and activities that are most appropriate to the ages and interests of the children they serve. They recognize that children of different ages need different types of activities and materials to help them learn best. Good teacher-caregivers also understand that attention must be paid to the individual interests and background of each child. For example, although similar-aged children share basic common characteristics, they differ in their individual rates of growth and in their experiences.

Staff in high quality programs recognize that children and their development are best understood within the context of their family and culture. They understand that the quality of care and education provided to children depends on establishing close ties with parents and other family members. They know that good early childhood programs are a vital support to families in their all-important task of childrearing.

For more than 60 years, NAEYC has strived to improve the quality for programs for young children. In recent years, these efforts have led to the adoption of official position statements regarding criteria for high quality in early childhood programs (Bredekamp, 1987) and developmentally appropriate practice in programs serving children birth through age 8 (Bredekamp, 1987). These positions define the Association's philosophy and beliefs regarding quality in early childhood programs. This volume focuses on quality *implementation* by considering characteristics that enhance or detract from a program's ability to provide high quality services to young children and their families.

The aspects that most influence a program's ability to provide high quality services revolve around characteristics of the staff—number, qualifications, ability, dispositions, and stability—and characteristics of the environment. Each aspect is associated with costs, and the lack of resources that has characterized the early childhood field has led too often to compromising on these characteristics. As a result, we have compromised quality for children.

The aspects that most influence a program's ability to provide high quality services revolve around characteristics of the staff.

PARAMETERS OF THE
FULL COST OF QUALITY

NAEYC's Full Cost of Quality campaign is designed to build understanding and support for the need to provide quality for all children. Particular attention must be given to the programmatic aspects that enhance or detract from quality services. Four parameters must be addressed, including a program's ability to

1. Foster **good relationships between children and adults** by limiting group size and the number of children per adult, promoting continuity for children, and enhancing staff-parent relationships;

2. Ensure that educational personnel have **qualifications** reflecting the **specialized preparation and knowledge** needed to work effectively with young children and their families;

3. Provide **adequate compensation** (salaries and benefits) to attract and retain qualified staff; and

4. Establish an **environment that enhances children's ability to learn** in a safe and stimulating setting and **provides good working conditions** for adults.

As the diagram below depicts, when any of these four parameters falls short of professional recommendations for high quality, the overall quality for children and families may be impaired.

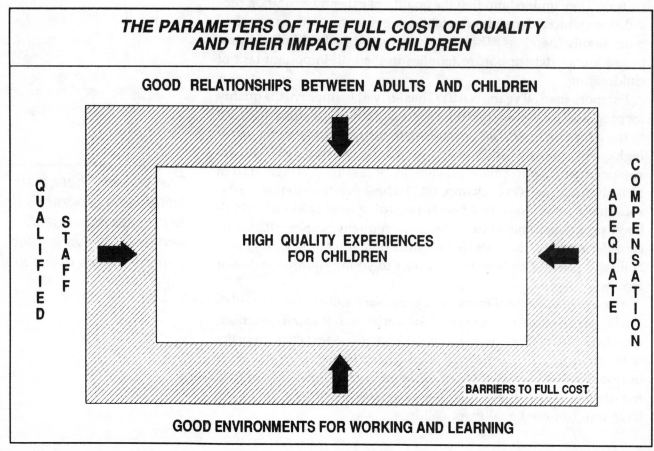

THE PARAMETERS OF THE FULL COST OF QUALITY AND THEIR IMPACT ON CHILDREN

GOOD RELATIONSHIPS BETWEEN ADULTS AND CHILDREN

QUALIFIED STAFF

HIGH QUALITY EXPERIENCES FOR CHILDREN

ADEQUATE COMPENSATION

BARRIERS TO FULL COST

GOOD ENVIRONMENTS FOR WORKING AND LEARNING

It should be noted that this definition does not include the provision of comprehensive support services. Such services have definite cost implications, and they are a vital component of quality when serving children and families who need assistance in acquiring basic resources. In some programs, all clients may have access to the basic resources of adequate food, health, shelter, and income. When these needs are not met, the early childhood program has a responsibility to help families gain access to needed services, through referral or service provision. It is only when basic needs are met that children and their families can fully benefit from the provision of a quality program. Thus, the costs of providing quality depend in part on the needs of the children and families served.

THE NEED FOR THE FULL COST OF QUALITY CAMPAIGN

Although more families than ever are relying on early childhood programs, there remains a pervasive lack of understanding of the benefits of such services, not just to families but to all of society. To date, the provision of early childhood services has been viewed as essentially a private arrangement between families and providers. Most early childhood programs depend primarily on parents to pay for services, but many families with young children have limited financial resources. Even with the significant expansion of federal assistance, the need is likely to remain high.

The lack of resources makes it difficult for programs to raise their prices. Limited program resources lead to inadequate compensation for staff, since personnel costs are the largest percentage of the program budget. Low wages and poor working benefits make it difficult to attract and retain qualified staff. Staff who remain in the field have little incentive to seek additional training and professional development. The early childhood professional shares a part of the responsibility for this vicious cycle by failing to adequately distinguish between the price that parents pay for services and the actual cost of service provision with adequately compensated staff.

An over-arching theme of this book is that the responsibility for early childhood care and education services is not limited to families, but that all of society has a stake in providing high quality services to our nation's youngest citizens. Only when we recognize that all sectors of society have a role and responsibility in supporting the care and education of young children, will we remove the barriers to full quality in early childhood programs.

The passage of a large federal child care bill, after some 20 years of effort, should provide a much needed boost to the early childhood field. Hopefully, the federal commitment will stimulate further investments by state and local governments and the private sector. Now that new funds are beginning to be seen, it is more important (and feasible) than ever to focus on ensuring program quality.

All of society has a stake in providing high quality services to our nation's youngest citizens.

A GROWING DEMAND FOR SERVICES BUT PUBLIC UNDERSTANDING LAGS

A growing demand

The recognition of federal responsibility for assisting in the provision of early childhood services has taken many years, and comes only following a tremendous growth in the demand for services. The increased demand has been greatest for infant, toddler, and preschool children. With over half of all mothers of preschool children now in the labor force, more and more families are relying on group programs—whether in centers or family child care—to provide supplemental care and education for their children. In addition to changing employment patterns of parents of young children, the increasing recognition of the value of early education has resulted in a greater number of preschool children attending group programs regardless of parental employment.

Policy makers have for the most part carefully distinguished between funds for programs serving primarily a "child care" function (that is, because parents are employed or otherwise unavailable) and those serving an "educational" function (to enhance a child's development). They have failed to realize that both aspects are important. The necessary ingredients for a good experience for children do not vary by the length of program day nor do they vary by setting. All good programs help children to learn and develop optimally and ensure that children are safe and well-cared for while not in the care of family members. Certainly, full work-day programs better meet the needs of employed parents who work from 9:00 to 5:00. Even among these families, many utilize multiple arrangements and may combine a part-time center program with care provided by a family child care provider.

A lack of understanding

The artificial separation of care and education stems from the historical reasons for which programs were first established (Kagan, 1988). Full work-day programs were generally begun to provide child care for employed mothers (typically single mothers with little income); part-day programs (including kindergarten and elementary school) emerged with an emphasis on social and educational experiences for children of families from middle and higher socioeconomic levels. The distinctions have blurred over time, primarily for two reasons. There has been increasing recognition of the benefits of early childhood programs for all children (and especially children living in poverty or otherwise at risk for school failure). Also, there has been a tremendous influx of mothers of young children into the labor force across all socioeconomic levels, prompting greater needs for child care. Yet, the dichotomy persists, in part because funding streams, delivery systems, and regulatory systems maintain bureaucratic distinctions.

The necessary ingredients for a good experience for children do not vary by the length of program day nor do they vary by setting.

Distinctions between care and education are typically linked to the child's age. Public perception tends to think in terms of "taking care" of younger children and "instructing" older children. Such definitions ignore younger children's capacity for learning and older children's need for care. The fact is that care and education are inexorably intertwined, not just for young children, but throughout childhood. The younger the child, the more the educational function must be embedded within the caregiving function, but the caregiving function remains important throughout childhood.

When we fail to recognize that children are learning from the day they are born, we also fail to provide a rich learning environment, and we deny children the opportunity for optimal growth and development. When we define education chiefly as an adult instructing a child, we ignore what is known about how children learn and emphasize intellectual development at the expense of the equally critical areas of social and emotional development. Although seldom recognized, public schools are the largest source of child care for school-age children during the hours in which the school operates. But, for many families, the part-day, part-year schedule of most schools fails to completely meet their needs for child care.

Maintaining the artificial dichotomy between care and education ignores recent knowledge, gained from research and practice, as to the processes of social, cognitive, and emotional development in the early childhood years and the ways in which such development may be enhanced through the skillful provision of appropriate learning environments. We now know that strategies for helping children learn must be developmentally appropriate, that is, they must be responsive to the child's age-related characteristics as well as her or his individual needs and interests. We know that children learn best when adults provide a rich environment which challenges children to actively manipulate materials and ideas that have relevance to their lives.

Regardless of program name—child care center, preschool, family child care, kindergarten, or primary grade—the general factors that determine the quality of the child's experience are the same, although the specific indicators of each factor will vary significantly by the age of child. For example, regardless of the program type or the child's age, an important goal is to foster a positive self-concept. For an adult working with infants, responding quickly to children's cries and holding and patting babies to provide comfort and stimulation is one appropriate strategy for reaching that goal. For school-agers, an appropriate strategy is quite different, such as providing opportunities for children to express their growing independence and self-reliance by making choices and initiating their own activities.

The younger the child, the more that education must be embedded within caregiving.

THE UNDERVALUING OF WORK WITH CHILDREN

The lack of understanding about the importance of the work of early childhood professionals in facilitating children's learning and supporting their families is set in the context of our nation's chronic indifference for young children. Such indifference is apparent in many ways. More young children are in poverty than are members of any other age group. Unlike other industrialized nations with generous children's allowances, paid parental leave, and universal access to quality preschool programs, the United States offers none of the above. Despite well-documented evidence about the long-term cost-effectiveness of such programs as prenatal health care, childhood immunizations, nutrition and feeding programs for mothers and children, and comprehensive early intervention services like Head Start, only a fraction of those eligible receive needed services. While the recent expansion of Head Start and the creation of a new child care program are significant steps in redressing these problems, we have a long way to go.

As a nation, we historically have placed less value on any type of work done for or with young children. Pediatricians earn less than other types of doctors. Kindergarten and elementary school teachers earn less than secondary school teachers. The problems are especially pervasive among early childhood professionals employed outside the public school, whether in centers or self-employed as family child care providers. The National Child Care Staffing Study (Whitebook, Howes, & Phillips, 1990) found that child care center teaching staff earned annual wages of less than one-half of those of comparably educated women in other professions and less than one-third of those of comparably educated men.

The primary reason that early childhood staff in programs outside the public school are grossly underpaid is that these program budgets generally are insufficient and do not allow adequate staff compensation. Parent fees are the primary source of income for many such programs, and low and moderate income parents are unable to afford the true costs of providing good service. This fact tends to depress the price of services, so that the price parents pay is often far below the actual cost of service provision, especially when adequate compensation is figured into the equation. Programs which receive public subsidies typically have been reimbursed at rates below the already depressed market rate, further undercutting program income. New guidelines for public subsidy attempt to address the market rate problem, but the wide variation in fees makes it difficult for higher quality programs (with higher costs) to be fully reimbursed for service.

As a result of the under-valuing of its work, the early childhood profession is caught in a vicious cycle. When a service is undervalued, its providers are inadequately compensated. The low compensation makes it difficult to recruit and retain highly trained staff.

Child care center teaching staff earn annual wages of less than one-half of those of comparably educated women in other professions and less than one-third of those of comparably educated men.

The fact that little financial incentive or reward is provided to early childhood professionals who want to continue to work with children limits the number seeking further training. The number of individuals who work in the field without professional qualifications contributes to the under-valuing of practitioners.

Given the importance of the early childhood years in shaping later development and learning and the increasing number of families relying on early childhood programs, it is crucial that such programs reflect existing knowledge concerning how best to provide care and education for our nation's youngest citizens. This means that all four parameters of full quality must be met.

Reaching the full cost of quality in early childhood programs will require breaking the vicious cycle of a lack of public understanding, inadequate public standards governing early childhood services, the lack of resources, inadequate compensation, high rates of turnover, and unacceptable quality for children. First and foremost, the public must understand the ingredients of quality in early childhood programs and be willing to pay their costs. Public standards related to the provision of quality services must be improved and rigorously enforced. Systems for providing training and professional development opportunities for service providers and for helping parents better access quality services need to be expanded and improved. Funds for service delivery and improvement also need to be expanded, with some funds targeted to increase the compensation provided to early childhood program staff.

Most important, the perception that parents alone are expected to bear the costs of providing early childhood programs must change. High quality early childhood programs benefit all sectors of society, now and in the future. It is time that the costs of their provision be borne more equitably by all segments of society. The good start in life that every child needs and deserves can only be achieved when the full cost of quality is paid for all children.

REFERENCES

Bredekamp, S. (Ed.). (1987). *Accreditation criteria and procedures of the National Academy of Early Childhood Programs.* Washington, DC: NAEYC.

Bredekamp, S. (Ed.). (1987). *Developmentally appropriate practice in early childhood programs serving children from birth through age 8,* expanded edition. Washington, DC: NAEYC.

Kagan, S.L. (1988). Current reforms in early childhood education: Are we addressing the issues? *Young Children, 43*(2), 27–32.

Whitebook, M., Howes, C., & Phillips, D. (1990). *Who cares? Child care teachers and the quality of care in America.* Final report of the National Child Care Staffing Study. Oakland, CA: Child Care Employee Project.

The good start in life that every child needs and deserves can only be achieved when the full cost of quality is paid for all children.

Current Price Versus Full Cost: An Economic Perspective

2

Mary L. Culkin, Suzanne W. Helburn, & John R. Morris

E ARLY CHILDHOOD professionals are all too familiar with the "trilemma" of providing affordable, available, quality child care. This chapter explains why market forces alone cannot be relied on to solve the trilemma, because of the special features of the market for early childhood care and education services. The cost of services make parents sensitive to the price they pay. Some parents lack the resources to pay for quality. Parents may have inadequate information about the complex of services they are purchasing and how important good services are to their child's development. The benefits from child care and early education are removed from the decision to buy the services by many years, and may accrue, at least in part, to society rather than to the child and family. Because the care and education of very young children has traditionally been provided at home, families are suffering something akin to automobile "sticker shock" as they adjust to the seemingly high market price of child care and education.

This chapter discusses the economics of early childhood care and education which underlie the trilemma, focusing on affordability and its effects on quality. We describe how child care and education costs are held down by a complex system of subsidies, some of which, such as low staff wages, are only now being recognized. Summarizing our recent research on the full production costs of early childhood services, we explore the effect of subsidies on affordability and quality. We close with a discussion of the policy implications of our research.

ECONOMIC TRENDS AND INCREASING NEEDS

Three trends account for the growth in early childhood care and education: the movement of women (especially mothers of young children) into the labor force; the increasing number of children who live in poverty; and the declining growth rate of the labor force. The child care trilemma is intensified by our growing recognition of the importance of early childhood experiences and learning to the healthy development of children.

It is becoming the norm in our society for mothers of young children to work outside the home, at least part-time, whether out of necessity or preference. This new norm affects patterns of family life and responsibilities for childrearing and early education. Families are

Market forces alone cannot solve the child care trilemma because of special features of the market for early childhood services.

increasingly purchasing services to care for and nurture their young, responsibilities previously fulfilled primarily by mothers at home. Thus, early childhood services are becoming a market commodity bought and sold according to principles of market demand and supply. Despite the increased use of purchased services, some services continue to be provided by parents, members of the child's extended family, or very close friends, so that market-based providers will always face some nonmarket competition.

Our nation is also experiencing a feminization of poverty. Women continue to earn substantially less than their male counterparts. Single mothers with children at home represent one of the fastest growing segments of our population; in these families, the mother's wages comprise most, if not all, of the family income. When mothers live in poverty, so do their children. Today, one out of every five children in the United States lives in poverty. Our children—the future generation of citizens, parents, and workers—are increasingly vulnerable to inadequate care, stimulation, and education resulting from limited financial resources. Children's early development is now often subject to market forces which control the provision of paid child care and education services.

A third trend is the changing demographic structure of the U.S. population, which affects the structure and quality of the labor force. The most dramatic recent change in our work force is its declining growth, due to the end of the baby boom. With fewer potential entrants and ongoing technological changes, our labor force will need every available worker to be more highly skilled than in the past. The increasing demands of technology make it especially important to address the needs of children in poverty, who are at higher risk of dropping out of the educational system and of acquiring fewer employment skills. Quality child care and education is an effective strategy to break the cycle of educational failure.

An economic perspective is useful for recognizing the powerful and irreversible forces that have operated during this century and have resulted in the continuous rise in labor force participation of women, particularly mothers of young children. The trend does not just reflect the increasing economic necessity or choice of mothers to work outside the home. It has also involved a shift from home to market production of consumer goods and services. This shift has supplied most of the market jobs which women have filled. The fact that we now characterize our economy as a service economy emphasizes the power of these trends; much of our economic growth reflects the shift in which, increasingly, businesses rather than families provide basic services.

Children's early development is now often subject to market forces which control the provision of paid care and education services.

THE ECONOMIC IMPORTANCE OF QUALITY CHILD CARE AND EDUCATION

The repercussions resulting from the widespread movement of mothers into the labor force—and the concomitant adjustments to family and community life—are comparable in their importance to those resulting from the advent of the automobile, which changed the face of the earth. These effects may be even more significant, because they affect our most intimate family relations and patterns, and ultimately, the structure of our society. Of all the social repercussions, moving to market-provided services for early childhood care and education may be the most problematic. It is one thing to buy processed foods and ready-made clothes, or to rely occasionally on fast foods; it is quite another to leave a very young child with someone outside the family for up to 50 hours a week.

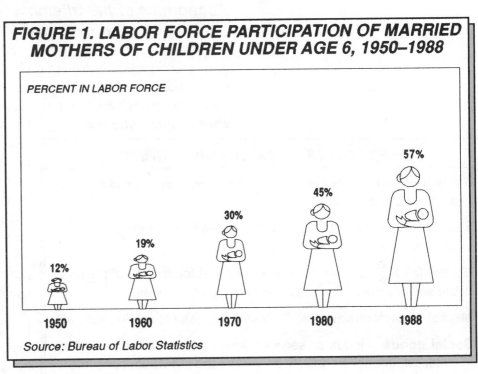

FIGURE 1. LABOR FORCE PARTICIPATION OF MARRIED MOTHERS OF CHILDREN UNDER AGE 6, 1950–1988

PERCENT IN LABOR FORCE

12% 1950
19% 1960
30% 1970
45% 1980
57% 1988

Source: Bureau of Labor Statistics

Child care is essential not only to children, but also to their parents and society when parents are employed. As depicted in Figure 1, the labor force participation rate for married women with children under six in the United States has increased from 12% in 1950 to 57% in 1988. Affordable, quality early childhood care and education is a crucial work-related service to families and their employers. As studies by Ellen Galinsky and others have documented (see Chapter 3), quality early childhood programs reduce parents' stress from juggling job and child-rearing responsibilities. Lower stress results in reduced absenteeism, tardiness, turnover, and recruiting costs as well as increased employee morale.

High quality early childhood services also help to create a more skilled future work force. Parents and policy makers are becoming increasingly aware of a relationship which educators have understood for some time—quality experiences during early childhood set the stage for later life. Thus, many parents enroll their preschool children in early childhood programs even when the mother is not employed.

The impact of quality care and education is especially significant for children "at risk" in terms of their social and educational development. Effective early intervention services can improve the likelihood that children will grow up to be productive members of society. Longitudinal research by the High/Scope Educational Research Foundation indicates that children who have attended a high quality early childhood program are significantly more successful in adult life. As adults, individuals who attended high quality preschool programs are more likely to have completed their high school educa-

Affordable, quality early childhood care and education is a crucial work-related service to families and their employers.

tion, to enroll in higher education programs, to be employed, and to have a stable family life. (Berrueta-Clement, Barnett, Schweinhart, Epstein, & Weikart, 1984).

Economics of the trilemma

Solving the trilemma of availability, affordability, and quality of services in early childhood care and education boils down, in large part, to economics. The three problems are interrelated and together they involve a trade-off between quality and quantity of services which in turn is based on costs. Quality affects costs, and therefore affordability. Affordability—how much families can pay for services—affects how much providers can charge. These constraints on fees, along with parents' and public perceptions of the characteristics of adequate early childhood services, determine the quality of services supplied. In a market economy, supply generally adjusts to demand. People can have the quality and amount of service they are willing or able to pay for. And, if we do not care much about the quality of service (for instance, if we are willing to leave children in their cribs or playpens or playgrounds or street corners to fend for themselves), we can eliminate the problem of availability. The fact is that high quality care (defined by some socially accepted standard) is not available at the prices many potential customers can afford to pay. The trilemma represents a vicious cycle caused by economic circumstances of both the purchasers and the suppliers of care.

Market failures and the demand for early childhood services

Market forces combine the desires of buyers with money (demand) and sellers of market services (supply), but market forces alone cannot solve the trilemma of affordability, availability, and quality. Economists explain the problem in terms of **market failure**: a situation in which market

---

DEFINITIONS OF ECONOMIC TERMS

Demand—the quantity and quality of services that families will buy at various prices

Supply—the quantity and quality of services that providers will offer at various prices

Market failure—a situation in which market forces do not provide the socially optimal quantity and quality of services

Market imperfections—factors which can lead to market failure

Social goods—goods or services which provide benefits to the wider community or society as well as the individual consumer

Merit goods—goods or services which provide more benefits to the consumer than the consumer recognizes

Income effect—the result when choice is limited by financial resources

Demand subsidies—resources provided for the purchase of services, allowing individual consumers to demand more or higher quality services than they could otherwise command

Supply subsidies—any gift, discount, or other contribution that allows suppliers to provide more services by lowering the costs of service provision

Redistributional subsidies—redistribute costs from one consumer to another, so that the lower fees paid by one client are subsidized by a higher paying client

Imputed costs—estimated costs of donated goods or services as if purchased at market price

Full cost of production—total cash expenditures plus in-kind donations plus foregone income of staff paid less than their market value

Market cost—total cash expenditures plus in-kind donations, but excluding the foregone income of underpaid staff

---

forces will not provide the socially optimal quantity and quality of services. In child care and education, market failures occur mainly on the demand side of the market. Because of the peculiarities of the demand for early childhood care and education services, families often do not or cannot buy enough quality care for their children. There are three major reasons for this market failure.

First, although both private and public needs are satisfied through the provision of good early childhood services, parents for the most part choose and pay for their children's care. Because the nature of young children's early experiences is so important to society, very much like public education, the quality of care can be considered too important to be based solely on family resources and preferences, allocated by market forces alone. In the jargon of economists, early childhood services are **social goods**. A good or service is a social good if, in addition to benefitting the purchaser, it also provides benefits to the wider community. Early childhood care and education is a social good, because it represents an investment in people which will benefit the society through providing a higher quality labor force (now and in the future) and preparing a more socially responsible citizenry.

Second, early childhood care and education services are **merit goods**. A merit good is any good or service which provides more benefits to the consumer than the consumer recognizes, so that she or he tends to buy less of it than she/he would with full information about its benefits. Early childhood care and education services are merit goods because of the complexity of the services being purchased combined with their high cost relative to family income. There is a broad spectrum of services and quality available, based partly on differing family desires (center, family child care, or the family home), differing needs, and parents' ability and willingness to pay. Consumers often do not have adequate information about the effect of differing quality programs on their children's development. In particular, the fact that services provide both care and education is not well understood. This information problem is exacerbated because the care and education of young children, previously provided primarily by mothers "for free," is undervalued by consumers. Furthermore, because some of the benefits of high quality child care are not felt until the child reaches or approaches adulthood, it is likely that parents will not appreciate these long-term benefits at the time of purchase and therefore will not assess them in determining how much quality to buy. Also, child care costs are high enough that families shop around for low-priced services, not necessarily realizing that they may be trading quality for lower fees. Parents with inadequate knowledge of care may choose lower priced services.

For many families, (especially, but not only, families in poverty), the high cost of care relative to their income may require them to accept lower costs and hence lower quality care for their children, even if they have adequate knowledge of quality differences. This **income effect** of choosing higher quality care is a third reason for

Early childhood care and education services are social goods because they are an investment which benefits the society.

under-purchasing of care by parents. Many families find it a struggle to feed and house their children, let alone pay for quality care. This income effect creates the basis for a two-tier system of care. To the extent that the lower quality care may lead to differential achievement of children in school, it institutionalizes income-based differences in achievement due to inadequate investment in the early development of children, especially those from low and moderate income families. While technically not a market failure, the income effect is an equity question. Families with fewer economic resources do not have the luxury of choosing what is best for their children.

This series of market problems creates a potential conflict over who should pay for child care. Even though the services are a social good, some of those who have been enjoying a free ride (the public and current and future employers), fail to recognize this fact and see no need to share in paying the costs. Young families, struggling financially and lacking full information about the impact on their children, try to minimize the costs of child care in order to retain the full benefits of working for pay. Providers, trying to attract customers through low fees, reduce quality. Some of the losses from lower quality services are not immediately apparent and may be borne by society in the form of children's decreased educational achievement or adults' impaired emotional adjustment. Because families do not incur immediate losses from choosing low quality care and may not recognize the long-term consequences, they cannot be expected to choose higher quality at a higher cost. The fact that society benefits from high quality early childhood services justifies public expenditures for their provision, either to increase families' ability to pay or to reduce their costs. This justification parallels the rationale for public expenditures for elementary, secondary, and higher education.

PROBLEMS AFFECTING THE MARKET IN EARLY CHILDHOOD SERVICES

DEMAND	SUPPLY
• Lack of information regarding characteristics of quality	• Highly competitive, volatile market
• Most evident benefits are long-term and accrue to society more than families	• Regulated services undercut by unregulated services
• Costs of poor quality not immediately apparent	• Workers willing to work for wages below the value of their services
• Quality services not affordable for many families	

The supply of early childhood services

In addition to the effect of demand-related market problems, there are peculiar characteristics related to supply—the ability of providers to develop and maintain a reliable stream of quality services. These are not market failures, but they do affect the way supply responds to demand. As already implied, if market forces allocate child care and education services, then providers can only provide what families demand. In this sense, there is always a balance of supply and demand. But, supply is limited to what consumers will pay for. To a large extent the quality of services is constrained by costs, which in turn are affected by the competitive characteristics of the industry.

Although paid child care provision outside the home has a long history, these services have been organizing into an "industry" or market only recently. This young industry is both volatile and highly competitive. For instance, in Denver in the first five months of 1990, over 250 new providers registered with the local resource and referral (R & R) service, while almost that many closed their doors. There is a diverse structure of private for-profit and non-profit providers. Business structure in the for-profit sector ranges from family child care provided by a woman in her own home to national corporate chains. The market is highly competitive. Not only do large centers compete with home-based family providers, but regulated (licensed) businesses compete with unregulated providers. In the unregulated sector there are virtually no financial barriers to starting up a business. Thus, both rapid growth and rapid turnover are characteristic.

Because of the high degree of competition, there are low mark-ups over costs in the for-profit sector, and constant threats to the competitive edge that a particular provider might temporarily enjoy. These competitive conditions create pressure on providers to reduce costs. Since labor costs represent about two-thirds of total costs, the main ways to cut costs are to pay lower wages, reduce the number of staff, or increase the number of children. Each of these strategies directly—and negatively—impacts the quality of the services provided. In addition, low wages and benefits lead to rapid staff turnover in centers, and uncertain profits create turnover in the supply of family child care homes and centers. Such instability hurts the quality of services received by children, as continuity of care is critical to children's development.

An interesting peculiarity of the market for early childhood services is the steady stream of workers, mainly women, who are willing to work for low incomes, despite their relatively high levels of education. It is not clear why early childhood teacher-caregivers are willing to work for wages that are so far below the value of their service, measured by wages in comparable occupations. The National Child Care Staffing Study, reporting average wages of $5.35 per hour, also found that real wages (adjusted for inflation) dropped 27% for teachers and 20% for assistants between 1977 and 1988 (Whitebook, Howes, & Phillips, 1989). Evidently, the willingness to work for less

It is not clear why early childhood teacher-caregivers are willing to work for wages that are so far below the value of their service.

than can be earned at other jobs is partly due to worker satisfaction with the work itself (Phillips, in press) and possibly because of a desire to make care affordable. To the extent that workers are uninformed about the economic cost they are incurring, this phenomenon represents a market failure which increases supply. More services are available at going prices than if child care employees were motivated purely by monetary reward. This willingness to work for low wages might erode over time if the labor market tightens and advocacy and professional organizations succeed in raising staffing standards.

To summarize our argument so far, the basic cause of the market problems in child care starts with the inability or unwillingness (perhaps due to poor information or separation of the action and its consequences) of families or society to demand enough quality services. Then, because of the competitive conditions and the complex nature of services, it is difficult for many providers to improve services on their own unless they have access to unique resources. Thus, the market will fail to provide sufficient high quality early childhood services if left to itself.

Subsidies in child care and education

The trilemma has always plagued early childhood care and education. The existing complex structure of programs offered by nonprofit and for-profit centers, schools, and family child care providers is the result of market and nonmarket forces that reflect responses to the perceived needs of children and the broader community. From the beginning, private charities setting up infant schools and kindergartens for the children of low-income working mothers understood the income effect of paying for care. Many forms of supply and demand subsidy have developed as a reaction to market failures, to offset the tendency to buy too little quality service.

Supply subsidies are any gift, discount, or other contribution that lowers the apparent cost of a particular service from what it would be if market costs were paid for all of its components. Supply subsidies make it possible to provide child care and education services and charge lower prices to all children. The most important supply subsidy is provided by early childhood teacher-caregivers. Other important supply subsidies include reduced or free occupancy charges (including rent, heat, electricity, and insurance), in-kind services, and cash reimbursements of services or supplies. Less

---

COMMON SUBSIDIES IN EARLY CHILDHOOD SERVICES

DEMAND
Provide partial or full payment of services

- scholarships
- grants
- government purchase of service
- tax credits for child care expenses
- vouchers for child care expenses

- -

SUPPLY
Gifts, discounts, or contributions toward the cost of program provision

- abnormally low staff wages in relation to qualifications
- reduced cost occupancy (space/facility costs)
- in-kind services
- cash reimbursements for costs of service provision not designated to cover costs of an individual child
- charitable or public program provision
- tax credits to establish or expand child care services

common, but also important, is the direct provision of charity or publicly supported programs. For example, programs such as Head Start directly increase the number of care and education spaces available. Some states have instituted tax credits to encourage employers to provide child care services, although with limited success. To the extent that such credits increase the supply of services, they represent a supply subsidy.

The biggest subsidy affecting fees for early childhood services is the abnormally low wages earned by program staff. This subsidy can be estimated two ways. One is to estimate the worth of the *job* based on wages in comparable jobs (e.g., elementary school teachers). The other is to estimate the market value of the *person*, or rather the person's services, (e.g., the average wages of women with similar levels of education for comparison). Either estimate may then be compared to the wages received by early childhood staff to determine the extent of subsidy that low wages represent.

Demand subsidies affect demand directly through partial or full payment of fees, allowing families to demand more or higher quality care—through scholarships, government subsidies, grants from United Way or other charitable private organizations, and tax credits for child care fees. Demand subsidies allow parents to afford more expensive care than they otherwise could obtain. The federal Dependent Care Tax Credit is the most prevalent example of a demand subsidy; several states also offer similar credits. The Dependent Care Tax Credit allows a family to claim a percentage of child care expenses as a credit toward the family's income tax payment, reducing the amount owed. Because the credit is nonrefundable, it only benefits families owing taxes. Therefore, it has been used mainly by middle income and prosperous customers. In 1990, the federal Earned Income Tax Credit, targeted to lower-income working families with young children, was greatly expanded. This may also be considered a demand subsidy, since the stated purpose of the increase was to provide child care assistance to the working poor. However, there are no requirements that the extra income received from the credit be used for child care purposes.

Direct demand subsidies that lower fees are generally specific to individual children and make it possible for their parents to enroll them in programs that are otherwise too expensive. Because demand subsidies provide assistance toward the purchase of service, they do not directly affect supply (the cost of production). Demand subsidies, therefore, do not directly affect the fees of non-subsidized children. Demand subsidies may, however, indirectly increase the fees of non-subsidized children by increasing the demand for child care resources.

Demand subsidies vary in their direct impact on programs. For example, vouchers or contracts are demand subsidies, whether paid for by the government or a private employer. Because they are

Demand subsidies vary in their direct impact on programs.

specifically for the purchase of early childhood services, the program automatically receives the full value of the subsidy at the time the services are purchased. However, demand subsidies in the form of tax credits for child care expenses do not pay for services directly; rather, parents pay the fees and then get a reduction in taxes or an increase in their tax refund the following year. Since the timing of the subsidy on vouchers or grants occurs at the time of purchase, these subsidies provide for an increase in demand. In the case of tax credits, there are at least three reasons why they might not influence demand for high quality care as much as direct subsidies. For families with a higher income who are eligible for the Dependent Care Tax Credit, there is no credit for fees over the effective limit of $200 per month per child, which is lower than the price many families already pay. Therefore, there is no incentive to pay higher fees for higher quality services. Second, families might compartmentalize decisions: they might not think about the tax credit at the time they make decisions about child care, and simply treat the credit (either the Dependent Care Tax Credit or the Earned Income Tax Credit) as a windfall to be spent on something else. Finally, if families do not have the purchasing power to buy the services desired (especially in the case of those receiving the Earned Income Tax Credit), the credit is irrelevant to their decisions.

Because direct demand subsidies usually benefit low-income families and tax credits benefit families with taxable income, the choice of subsidy is particularly important from a policy perspective. Since the mid-1970s, the predominant form of federal child care assistance has shifted from reliance on the direct purchase of services (primarily through Title XX and the Social Services Block Grant) to use of the federal tax credit. Between 1977 and 1988 federal Title XX spending for child care declined by almost 60% in constant dollars; during the same period the child care tax credit increased four-fold in constant dollars, so that it represented 60% of all federal spending on child care (Robins, 1990). As a result, federal policies in the 1980s shifted aid toward middle-class families and away from low-income families. However, the tax credit subsidy per child is a small percentage of families' child care costs. Given the reasons already cited as to why the tax credit for expenses fails to influence demand, this government policy failed to correct the market failures affecting child care services. The increase in the Earned Income Tax Credit, designed to provide child care assistance, is also unlikely to correct market failures. However, the new federal child care block grant program also enacted in 1990, with $750 million allocated in the first year for improving child care affordability, supply, and quality, may well affect market forces, because it includes direct demand and supply subsidies.

In addition to supply and demand subsidies, there are also **redistributional subsidies**. Such subsidies exist when the costs for services are redistributed among clients, transferring some costs of service for one child to another within the center or home. Examples of redis-

To examine the importance of subsidies, we studied the relation between costs, revenue sources, and the quality of services in seven programs.

tributional subsidies include fee structures in which families pay the same rate for infants and toddlers as older children, even though it is more expensive to provide care for younger children, or in which higher-income families subsidize lower-income families. Discounts for second children in the same family served by a provider may redistribute costs to others attending the program. If the discounted fees are sufficient to cover the costs of the additional child and permit filling otherwise unfilled spaces, this pricing policy may in fact lower the average cost per child, because the added income is greater than the expense of providing service even at the lower rate.

THE IMPORTANCE OF SUBSIDIES: RESULTS OF OUR RESEARCH

To examine the importance of subsidies, we studied the relation between costs, revenue sources, and quality of services in seven early childhood care and education programs in Colorado. The seven sites included two family child care homes, three nonprofit centers, one Head Start program, and one proprietary (for-profit) infant center. The sites were chosen to reflect the diversity of service providers. Four program types were of interest: programs receiving virtually complete public support, other nonprofit centers, family child care homes, and for-profit centers. A case study approach was utilized, purposefully examining a limited number of programs in great depth. Results were averaged for program types when they were represented by more than one site (nonprofit centers and family child care homes). Since the findings are based on only a few sites, these results should not be interpreted as representative of the actual service costs for an entire sector of the market or types of programs. These findings are, however, illustrative of the differential effects of various subsidies and the impact of the fact that different program types have differential access to subsidy.

We assessed overall program quality through on-site observation using the Harms and Clifford Early Childhood Environmental Rating Scale (ECERS), Infant Toddlers Environmental Rating Scale (ITERS), or Family Day Care Rating Scale (FDCRS) (Harms, Clifford, 1980, 1989; Harms, Clifford, and Cryer, 1989). Data on costs, revenues (including in-kind donations, fund-raising efforts, etc.), staffing ratios, and the professional preparation of staff, were collected through interviews with center directors or family child care providers. We developed a spread sheet model of actual costs, including the imputed costs of in-kind and volunteer services. The model was used to estimate full production costs per child per month for the

---

DIFFERENT WAYS OF MEASURING COSTS IN EARLY CHILDHOOD PROGRAMS

Full cost of production—a program's total cash expenditures, plus in-kind donations, including the foregone income of staff who are paid less than their market value

Market cost—cost per child if all supply subsidies except the low wage subsidy are included in the cost estimate

Cash cost—excludes the value of in-kind donations and estimates the actual cash outlay of the provider

Apparent cost—excludes the value of all supply subsidies

center or home, the percentage of costs covered by supply and demand subsidies and in-kind or volunteer contributions, and the relation between fees and full production costs. The full production costs (cash outlay plus imputed value of in-kind donations, including those from low staff wages) varied considerably, ranging from $459 per child per month for one family provider to more than $1,148 per child per month for the infant care center.

Quality was related to cost, but not in a simple way. While high total costs did not necessarily mean high quality, high education levels for staff were related to quality and also tended to raise costs. Nevertheless, low wages were important in keeping fees down, especially in high quality sites. High occupancy costs were related to more expensive or more expansive facilities, but did not correlate highly with the quality of care. High subsidies did seem to correlate with high quality.

One of the problems tackled in this study was to distinguish between different ways to measure cost. Actual cash outlays of centers and homes do not represent the full cost of care if there are in-kind donations, such as those from the staff in the form of low wages, or rent reductions. Furthermore, cash outlays may be paid for by cash donations. Table 1 shows four different measures of the cost of production and one way of measuring costs to parents. The **full cost**

TABLE 1. FOUR MEASURES OF PROVIDER COST COMPARED TO FEES FROM PARENTS BY TYPE OF SETTING

	One Head Start Program*	Average of 3 Nonprofit Centers	Average of 2 Family Child Care Homes	One For-profit Infant Center
Full Production Cost *(at comparable worth)*	$548	$687	$502	$1,148
Market Costs *(at actual low wages)*	$472	$458	$288	$613
Cash Costs *(excluding in-kind donations)*	$406	$404	$243	$613
Apparent Costs *(excluding all supply donations)*	$18	$333	$199	$613
Fees from Parents or Others	$3	$204	$185	$613

*The main sources of revenue are the Head Start program are the Head Start and related grants which we have treated as supply donations because they are grants to the provider.
Source: Colorado University at Denver Economics Department

of production represents a program's total cash expenditures, plus in-kind donations, including the foregone income of staff who were paid less than their market value. **Market cost** represents cost per child if all supply subsidies are included in the cost estimate except the low wage subsidy. **Cash cost** excludes the value of in-kind donations and estimates the actual cash outlay of the provider. The last cost estimate, **apparent cost**, excludes the value of all supply subsidies. This estimate represents the costs that need to be covered by parent fees and demand subsidies. Fees from parents represent out-of-pocket costs at the time of purchase of services. Fees somewhat over-estimate actual parental costs because they ignore the effect of tax credits for child care expenses.

Table 2 presents this information in a slightly different way. It shows the cumulative effect of all the subsidies by type. In our study, the combined effect of all subsidies for the average nonprofit center was to reduce the effective price to parents (fee less federal income tax credit) from a full production cost of $687 per month to $149 per

TABLE 2. RELATION BETWEEN FULL PRODUCTION COST, SUBSIDIES, AND THE COST TO THE PARENT BY TYPE OF SETTING

	Cost per Child per Month			
	One Head Start Program	Average of 3 Nonprofit Centers	Average of 2 Family Child Care Homes	One For-Profit Infant Center
Full Production Costs	$548	$687	$502	$1,148
Less: Supply Subsidies				
Low wage subsidy	76	234	214	535
In-kind subsidy	66	54	45	0
Cash supply subsidy	388	46	44	0
Deficit in nonprofit centers		19		
Cost after Supply Subsidies	$18	$333	$199	$613
Less: Demand Subsidies				
Cash demand subsidies	19	129	14	0
Income tax credit	0	55	46	40
Net Cost to Parent*	$3	$149	$139	$573

*Net Cost to Parent may exceed cost after all subsidies if center has a surplus for the year.
Source: Colorado University at Denver Economics Department

month. Supply side subsidies included the effect of low wages, in-kind donations to the center, and some cash donations (including the federal grant to the Head Start program). Deficits being incurred by the nonprofit centers were included with the supply subsidies. Demand subsidies included support for individual children and family income tax credits.

The Head Start program was targeted to low-income families, as were two of the three nonprofit centers. One of the two family child care homes served a lower middle-income clientele. The remaining programs served middle- to upper-income families. Except for the subsidy of foregone staff wages (received by all providers), only those programs serving lower income families received supply subsidies. All programs received indirect demand subsidies through the federal Dependent Care Tax Credit. Programs serving lower income families were also eligible for direct demand subsidies provided through the state purchase of care and United Way.

The high net cost to parents in the infant center ($573) resulted from two factors. First, serving infants requires more staff and incurs higher costs. Second, this program had a middle-income clientele and was a for-profit center. The only subsidies available to it were the foregone wages of staff and the subsidy provided by the federal tax credit for child care expenses.

Since our study design is a case study approach, the sample was limited and not representative. We do not know if our cost estimates would be replicated in other studies. We do know that different types of programs qualify for different subsidies, depending on tax status and clientele and that costs vary widely. These results show the great variation in production costs, subsidies, and fees between different types of programs and for different clients. These cases illustrate the effects of this wide variation in subsidies on costs and fees.

Table 2 shows two important phenomena. First, because of the large subsidy in the form of low wages of child care staff, no families paid anywhere near the full production costs of child care. Second, the subsidies varied greatly from child to child and center to center, based partly on the family income and partly on the ability of the program to generate subsidies. In the Head Start program, the total subsidies exceeded 99% of the cost. In the other three nonprofit centers, the total subsidies exceeded 75% of cost. In the two homes, subsidies averaged 70%, and in the proprietary infant center they were almost 50%. It should be noted that the average subsidy for the three nonprofit centers masks substantial differences in the type and absolute level of subsidy.

Supply side subsidies reduced the production cost of providing the child care service. These included low wages relative to the quality of the worker, USDA food reimbursement (available to nonprofit centers and family child care homes), charitable gifts, and in-kind donations. Low wages reduced costs in these sites between $76 and $535

We found that subsidies were not evenly available to all programs.

per month per child. The in-kind donations of space and other items reduced costs by $19 to $81 per month per child for the centers which received them. The USDA food program (a cash subsidy), where applicable, reduced average costs by $29 to $48 per month per child; other cash donations reduced costs by smaller amounts.

Demand side subsidies increased the parents' ability to pay the fees for the care demanded. Demand subsidies varied from 6.5% of cash revenue for tax credits received for child care expenses in the proprietary center to over 70% of cash revenue in one center where reimbursement for state purchase of care and United Way contributions were particularly high.

Redistributional subsidies were not important for these sites. Older children often attended different centers than did infants. In the center where the two age groups were both present, differences in tuition closely reflected the difference in cost. Where sliding fee scales based on income existed, reduced fees for children from low-income families were usually financed by scholarship funds from outside contributions, not from fees of other children. Inadequate reimbursement of expenses for children covered by the state purchase of care was financed by contributions from other sources, not from tuition differentials. There were very few second children in the centers we examined. Although subsidies related to pricing policy are possible, it may be that competition is keen enough to discourage redistributing costs between clients. Raising the price for one child in order to lower it for another may create the risk of losing the higher paying client and the subsidy.

We found that subsidies were not evenly available to all programs. While all the programs in our sample utilized the subsidy of undercompensated staff, other supply subsidies (charitable gifts or in-kind donations) were available primarily to nonprofit programs. Demand subsidies, including those provided through state purchase of care, were available to clients of all programs, but some programs received fewer demand subsidies because they did not enroll children from low-income families.

Federal and state governments are already involved in the provision of child care services through purchase of care subsidies for some low-income families and income tax credits for the middle class. As this study shows, the federal subsidy to the middle class is small in the individual amounts received, but systematic in that any family with a tax liability can receive it. The subsidy for low-income families is uneven because funds are inadequate to serve all that apply, and the public reimbursement is less than the market price. Unequal opportunities for children from low-income families are exacerbated by the fact that limited public subsidies are supplemented by local sources in some communities but not in others. The good news is that subsidies can increase the quality, affordability, and availability of early childhood services. The bad news is that current subsidies

Our research shows that supply and demand subsidies can be used to make high quality early childhood services "affordable" to families.

depend most on underpaid staff. And, even when the subsidy provided through inadequate wages is counted, there are insufficient subsidies to provide assistance to all who need it in order to obtain good services.

REFLECTIONS AND POLICY DISCUSSION

Our cost modeling study indicates that some children from low-income families are receiving good quality care, perhaps because subsidies increase the quality of care in some centers intended to serve low-income families. The present system allows pockets of quality care to develop, but does not provide systematic provision of quality services for all children. As suggested by the results of the National Child Care Staffing Study (Whitebook et al. 1989), the squeeze between quality and cost is increasingly felt by middle income families who are too well off to qualify for subsidies beyond the federal tax credit but who cannot afford the higher costs of quality programs.

Our study demonstrates the complexity of the relationship between quality and cost. In our sample, the most expensive programs, whether defined by parent fees or production costs, were not always the best in terms of program quality. However, programs which demonstrated the highest levels of program quality had staff with the most years of education. This finding corroborates the results of the National Child Care Staffing Study (Whitebook et al., 1989) and other research documenting the relationship between levels of staff preparation and program quality. Because of inadequate wages, the costs of staff with higher educational levels does not always show up in higher fees or market costs and is only apparent when the value of foregone wages is added into the equation.

Our findings indicate that there is considerable variation in the fees paid by parents and, hence, affordability of early childhood services. In part, the variation is due to differences in subsidies in different child care settings and among different income levels. If this variation based on auspice and subsidies exists generally, and we have no reason to believe otherwise, then this study indicates how misleading it can be to describe costs and fees for early childhood services in terms of averages. The greater the variance from the average figure, the more significant the differences in the financial burden for individual families. This variation needs to be taken into account in forming public policy. The often cited $3,000 "average" cost of child care is a perfect example. Even if this figure reflects the average price that families pay for child care services nationally, it obscures the fact that some families are paying three times that amount.

Most important, our research shows that supply and demand subsidies can be used to make high quality care and education "affordable" to families. Only through the use of such subsidies, are the market failures inherent in the provision of early childhood

When we let market forces prevail, the nation is deprived of the benefits of all young children receiving quality early childhood services.

services likely to be overcome. While there might also be ways to make more efficient use of available monies and still maintain quality, there is no research evidence to suggest what these options might be.

A major reason for market failures in early childhood care and education is inadequate information and coordination of demand and supply. The development of comprehensive resource and referral organizations which is now occurring in many communities should be encouraged as a way to increase market efficiency. On the demand side, R & Rs are a source of needed information for consumers. They perform vital educational functions by informing parents about quality issues related to the services they buy, and they can also help families access demand subsidies for which they qualify. By informing businesses and the general community about the benefits of quality care and education programs, R & Rs foster greater understanding of early childhood services as a merit good, and hence the need for public support. The information that they can generate about the supply and demand for quality services can stimulate both the public and private sectors to provide needed demand subsidies.

Resource and referral services can also help supply respond to demand. They help recruit and train new providers. By publicizing the existence of regulations and their relation to the quality of care provided, R & Rs can encourage use of regulated services and promote the adoption of improved regulatory standards. Acting as a "broker" between service providers and potential sources of funding, R & Rs often stimulate improvements and expansion of service provision. Many exemplary public-private partnerships to improve child care affordability, quality, and availability revolve around the services provided by R & Rs. Given their unique mediating position, resource and referral organizations are in a good position to respond to future trends likely to affect early childhood service supply and demand. For all of these reasons, R & Rs need to be supported in public and private efforts to improve the match between supply and demand for quality early childhood services.

Child care costs will increase if the pay for early childhood program staff begins to approximate pay in other occupations. We project that wages and benefits will rise, because of existing difficulties in recruiting qualified staff and the projected tightening of the labor market, which will encourage more qualified women into higher paying occupations. For some centers, wages will rise immediately as the new minimum wage is implemented.

It is unlikely that the early childhood industry will be able to continue counting on a sufficiently large cadre of qualified individuals to keep wages at their present depressed level. In addition to the tightening labor market, greater understanding of the economic effects of accepting low wages may create pressure to raise wages. Also, as early childhood staff achieve more professional status through higher levels of skills and preparation, wages should rise to reflect the increased quality of services.

It is unlikely that the early childhood industry will be able to continue counting on a sufficiently large cadre of qualified individuals to keep wages at their present depressed level.

If these pressures on cost materialize, it will be all the more important to devise a more coherent system of subsidies which address questions of fairness and efficiency. This system might well include incentives to promote business as well as philanthropic and municipal subsidies. Overdependence on market allocation will make quality care all the more unavailable to low-income families and those who lack understanding of the importance of early childhood education. Failure to intervene will mean sacrificing quality care for many of our nation's youngest citizens. Quality care and education is a social good, benefitting not just the child and family but all of society. When we let market forces prevail, the nation is deprived of the benefits of all young children receiving quality early childhood services and being better prepared to become more effectively functioning members of society.

REFERENCES

Berrueta-Clement, J. R., Barnett, W. S., Schweinhart, L. J., Epstein, A.S., & Weikart, D. P. (1984). *Changed lives—The effects of the Perry Preschool Program on youths through age 19.* Ypsilanti, MI: The High/Scope Educational Research Project.

Harms, T., & Clifford, R. M. (1980). *Early Childhood Environment Rating Scale.* New York and London: Teachers College, Columbia University.

Harms, T., & Clifford, R. M. (1989). *Family Day Care Rating Scale.* New York and London: Teachers College, Columbia University.

Harms, T., Cryer, D., & Clifford, R. M. (1989). *Infant/Toddler Environment Rating Scale.* New York and London: Teachers College, Columbia University.

Phillips, D. (in press). Child care as an adult work environment: Implications for job satisfaction, turnover, and quality of care. *Journal of Social Issues.*

Robins, P. K. (1990, May). *Child care policy and research: An economist's perspective.* Paper presented at the Carolina Public Policy Conference, The Economics of Child Care, University of North Carolina at Chapel Hill.

Whitebook, M., Howes, C., & Phillips, D. (1989). *Who cares? Child care teachers and the quality of care in America.* Executive summary of the National Child Care Staffing Study. Oakland, CA: Child Care Employee Project.

The Costs of *Not* Providing Quality Early Childhood Programs

3

Ellen Galinsky

T HE DEBATE in this country has shifted from the issue of whether or not mothers of young children should be employed to a recognition that they are—and will continue to be in the labor force in even greater numbers. Concurrently, there has been a realization that child care responsibilities cannot be placed on families alone, but that both the private and the public sectors have a role in supporting quality early childhood programs. Rather than ask "why" they should be involved, increasingly businesses, governments, and charitable organizations are asking "how" they can help.

In these discussions, decision makers frequently turn to research to guide their efforts. If there is any one clear message to be drawn from the research on child care and early education, it is that the quality of programs has a definite and lasting effect on children's development. This chapter summarizes what is known about the ingredients of quality in early childhood arrangements and their effects on children, their parents, and their teacher-caregivers. In addition, this chapter presents what is known about the cost of *not* providing quality.

THE EFFECT OF QUALITY ON CHILDREN

The importance of relationships

The personal relationship

The most important ingredient of quality is the relationship between the child and the teacher-caregiver, whether the setting is in a center, a family child care home, or the child's home. This is why NAEYC's accreditation process for early childhood programs places great emphasis on the nature of the interactions between teachers and children. Parents also understand the importance of relationships. Parents report that the kind and quality of the attention their child receives strongly affects their decision in selecting one arrangement over another (Galinsky, 1988).

Children do form attachments to their teacher-caregivers, although Thomas Gamble and Edward Zigler (1986), in a review of this research, remind us that children's attachments to their parents are pre-eminent. Carollee Howes from the University of California at Los Angeles and her colleagues have found that children with a secure attachment to their mothers *and* their teacher-caregiver behave more

Parents report that the kind and quality of attention their child receives strongly affects their choice of an early childhood program.

competently than those with two or more insecure attachments (Howes, Rodning, Galluzzo, & Myers, 1988). Thus, it seems, the cost we could pay for poor relations between the child and the teacher-caregiver is the child's feeling that she or he is just one of the crowd and not a special, unique individual. A good self-concept is one of the foundations of emotional and social well-being. The costs may be very high, especially in terms of children's ability to form healthy relationships with others and enjoy good emotional health.

The teaching relationship

No matter what the setting—center, family child care, or the child's home, teacher-caregivers are teaching children every moment, both formally and informally. The way this teaching is done makes a difference in children's development. For example, a study by Deborah Phillips, Kathleen McCartney, and Sandra Scarr (1987) found that when children are talked to, asked questions, and encouraged to express themselves, their social development is enhanced: They are more likely to be considerate. In fact, the children in this study were also rated as more intelligent and task-oriented. The teaching environment was found to be more predictive of the children's achievement than their social class background. Kathleen McCartney (1984), in a re-analysis of this same data set, found that when children were in a verbally stimulating environment, they were more likely to achieve on tests of cognitive abilities and language development.

Early childhood specialists voice concern over situations in which children are either bored or pressured. In a longitudinal study, Deborah Lowe Vandell and her colleagues found that 4-year-olds who attended programs in which they spent time aimlessly wandering around were more likely at 8 years of age to have developmental problems, including less acceptance by peers, less social competence, and poorer conflict resolution skills (Vandell, Henderson, & Wilson, 1988).

Marcy Whitebook, Carollee Howes, and Deborah Phillips, in their landmark National Child Care Staffing Study (1990), found that children were more likely to be engaged in aimless wandering in programs with high rates of staff turnover. This key signal of lower program quality was associated with programs offering lower staff salaries, fewer benefits, and poorer working conditions. These researchers detected immediate negative consequences of poorer program quality. Children in such programs did less well on tests of both social development and language development, critical areas for later achievement.

Just as children do less well when they are bored or wandering aimlessly, David Elkind from Tufts University (1987), has pointed to the potential for problems such as elementary school burnout when preschool children are overly pressured. Thus, the cost we could pay for inadequate teaching relationships in children's early years is great: diminished achievement and poorer social and language skills.

No matter what the setting, children are being taught every moment, both formally and informally.

The disciplinary relationship

There has been a great deal of research indicating that the disciplinary techniques parents use have an impact on the child's subsequent development. These findings can be applied to early childhood programs. Children are more likely to develop self-control and to become more compliant, cooperative, and considerate of others if reasoning is used; if teacher-caregivers explain how a child's behavior affects others; and if problem-solving skills are taught. Vandell and Powers (1983) found that in higher quality programs, children had many more positive interactions with staff than in lower quality programs. Finkelstein (1982) showed that when teacher-caregivers are trained in behavior management techniques, the frequency of children's aggressive acts is reduced.

Such research counters the societal fear that attendance in group programs itself leads to more aggression in children. The ways that teacher-caregivers (or parents) handle young children's aggression can lead to greater or reduced aggression. The difference lies in understanding how to deal with children's aggression in appropriate ways. Lesser quality programs are more likely to have staff who do not have the knowledge and understanding to deal effectively with young children's normal assertions of prowess and power. The cost that we as a society could pay for children who grow up more aggressive seems high indeed.

The stability of relationships

With 40% of all center staff and 60% of all in-home providers leaving the field every year, it is no wonder that one 4-year-old recently said to a teacher, "I don't have to listen to you. I was here before you came and I'll still be here when you leave." Other parents report their children resist going to child care because they simply don't know who will care for them that day. According to the research of Mark Cummings from West Virginia University (1986), children have a much easier time separating from their mothers when they are cared for by well-known teacher-caregivers in small groups. Carollee Howes and her colleagues, in their studies of family child care (Howes & Stewart, 1987), found that there was a cost to children who changed arrangements frequently: They were less competent in their interactions with materials and with other children. As previously described, the National Child Care Staffing Study (Whitebook et al., 1990) documented disturbing results for children's social and language development when they were enrolled in programs with high rates of staff turnover. The Staffing Study also painted a disturbing picture of the amount of turnover in programs. Based on initial reports of program directors, the study found a 41% annual turnover rate, comparable to other nationally reported figures. However, the researchers found a 37% turnover rate in just over 6 months, based on the results of follow-up calls.

Children in centers with high staff turnover demonstrate poorer skills in language development and social development.

The resources of child care

The second aspect of early childhood program quality relates to the program's resources: the group size, adult-child ratio, health and safety considerations, and the professional preparation of teacher-caregivers.

Group size and staff-child ratio

The federal government funded the National Day Care Study in the late 1970s to investigate the degree to which the regulated features of child care arrangements had an effect on children's development. One of their most important findings was that the group size made a big difference in program quality. In smaller groups the adults spent more time being with children and less time simply watching them. The children were more verbal, more involved in activities, and less aggressive. Finally, the children in smaller groups made the greatest gains in standardized tests of learning and vocabulary (Ruopp, Travers, Glantz, & Coelen, 1979).

The National Day Care Study did not find staff-child ratio as powerful as group size in predicting development for children 3 to 5 years of age. However, the range they examined was limited. As Deborah Phillips and Carollee Howes point out (1987), "The majority of studies have found that the [adult-child] ratio has a significant effect on adult and child behavior in child care." More recently the National Child Care Staffing Study (Whitebook et al. 1990) found that fewer children per caregiver was associated with more developmentally appropriate activities. Teachers in these groups were more sensitive, less harsh, and less detached when interacting with children. The number of children per adult has obvious consequences for the ability of the caregiver to be responsive to each child. The younger the children and the more dependent they are on adults, the more critical it is that the number of children per adult be limited. The crucial learning from this research is that adult-child ratios and group size must be considered together.

Health and safety

There has been a great deal of public concern about the transmission of illness in child care. Susan Aronson has been studying the health risks in group programs for the past decade. She has found a clear demarcation between those early childhood programs in which children often become ill and those in which they do not: When adults wash their hands frequently, children are healthier (Aronson, 1987). The costs of children's illness and injury are obvious in health care expenses and missed days of work for their parents.

Children's safety is another critical factor to consider. Children's safety can be improved when providers are knowledgeable and when the environment is hazard reduced. Safety is also enhanced when ratios and group size are limited. Currently 19 states permit ratios of 5 or more infants to each adult (Adams, 1990). These ratios must be questioned not only in terms of their costs on the relationships

The costs of an unsafe environment are incalculable when children's lives are at stake.

established between teacher-caregivers and children, but also for their costs in safety. The extra attention afforded by small groups and good ratios helps to prevent minor accidents and injuries. It may be a life-saver in cases of emergency evacuation. The costs of an unsafe arrangement are incalculable when children's lives are literally at stake.

Teacher-caregiver preparation and training

NAEYC's experience with its accreditation system has documented that developmentally appropriate teaching practices and activities are more likely to occur when staff have a combination of formal education and specific preparation in early childhood education (Bredekamp, 1989). Other research is mixed regarding the specific characteristics of professional preparation that most contribute to program quality. The National Day Care Study (Ruopp et al., 1970) concluded that one of the most important ingredients of quality was the ongoing, relevant training of providers. In programs in which teacher-caregivers had specific early childhood training, the children behaved more positively, were more cooperative, and were more involved in the program. These children also made the greatest gains on standardized tests of learning. The National Child Care Staffing Study (Whitebook et al., 1990) suggested that the formal education of staff was a more potent predictor of program quality than early childhood training alone. While more research is needed to better define the specific relationships between different types and amounts of preparation and quality, the overall message of the importance of specialized knowledge is clear.

In summary, research on the impact of the resources of the child care program reveals a strong connection between group size, staff-child ratios, health and safety, and staff development and children's social, physical, and cognitive well-being.

Relationships with parents

Numerous studies have been conducted on the long-term effects of early childhood programs, especially model intervention programs and federally funded Head Start programs. One of the most noteworthy findings is that when early childhood programs are effective, they do much more than teach the child. The parents are affected and through this experience become better teachers, motivators, and advocates for their children (Lally, Mangione, & Honig, 1987; Weikart, 1990). This is not happenstance; providing meaningful opportunities for parental involvement has been an integral part of Head Start throughout its 25-year history.

A recent follow-up study of Head Start in Philadelphia (Copple, Cline, & Smith, 1987) is noteworthy in that it reflects typical rather than exemplary programs. In that study, Head Start children were more likely to avoid serious school problems, were less frequently retained, and had better attendance records than their counterparts

There is a strong connection between program characteristics such as group size, staff-child ratios, health and safety, and staff qualifications and children's social, physical, and cognitive well-being.

who did not attend the program. The researchers suggest that the Head Start program may have reduced the helplessness these parents felt in response to the school. Instead of seeing school as a place where their children were doomed, they may have come to see it as a place where their children could hold their own, and where they, as parents, could speak out on behalf of their children's education.

The importance of establishing good working relationships with parents is not universally understood. A recent study conducted by the Families and Work Institute sounds a warning signal about this critical aspect of quality care and education. We found that the parents most likely to have the best parent-teacher relationships were the wealthier, most advantaged parents. Similarly, those least likely to have good relationships—the least advantaged, minority parents— are those who could perhaps use the support the most (Galinsky, Shinn, Phillips, Howes, & Whitebook, 1990).

Summary of the effects of quality on children

The studies described throughout this chapter have been carefully controlled. The effects of different family backgrounds have been statistically accounted for so that the researchers could determine the impact of quality on children's development. The evidence is re-soundingly uniform. The quality of early childhood programs has a strong effect on children's development. Carollee Howes (1990) summarizes her numerous studies on different forms of child care by stating, "Children who entered low quality child care as infants were [the] least task oriented and considerate of others as kindergartners, had the most difficulty with peers as preschoolers, and were distractible, extroverted, and hostile as kindergartners."

THE EFFECTS OF QUALITY ON EMPLOYED PARENTS

While some of the costs of poor quality for children may not be readily apparent, we do not have to wait to assess the cost of child care problems on employed parents: The repercussions are showing up right now in diminished job performance.

An inadequate selection

It is difficult for parents to find quality child care. In a survey we conducted with 931 employees at three New Jersey companies (Galinsky, 1988), 46% of the respondents reported that locating quality arrangements was a "major problem"; 48% did not feel they had an adequate selection. Infant care was the most difficult to find—65% indicated that making arrangements for their infants was "difficult" or "very difficult."

A national study conducted by the National Council of Jewish Women (1988) of 1,927 women approximately 5 months after they had given birth found that new mothers who had problems arranging child care were more likely to experience higher levels of stress. In

Some of the costs of poor quality for children may not be readily apparent, but the repercussions for parents in diminished job performance are evident right now.

a nationally representative study conducted for *Fortune* magazine (Galinsky & Hughes, 1987), we found that parents who had trouble finding child care were more likely to have higher absenteeism rates.

Satisfaction

It is well known that it can be difficult for parents to admit that they are dissatisfied with the overall quality of child care even though they may admit displeasure with particular aspects of their arrangements. In the Parent/Teacher Study, conducted in conjunction with the National Child Care Staffing Study, we found that there are two sets of factors that parents use to make judgments about child care. One relates to the quality of the child's experience (the warmth of the teacher-caregiver, the activities, etc.). When parents are dissatisfied with this set of factors they are less likely to be satisfied with their child care arrangement in general. The second set of factors relates to the parents' experience with child care (hours, flexibility of scheduling, cost, location, and parents' opportunity for input). When parents are dissatisfied with these conditions, they are more likely to have higher levels of stress, more work-family conflict, and more stress-related health problems, but there is little effect on their overall satisfaction with the child care (Shinn, Galinsky, & Gulcur, 1990).

These new findings help to explain the seeming contradiction in earlier studies where overall satisfaction is reported at high levels, but considerable concern is expressed about specific factors. Parents voice the most concern with the factors that directly affect them: location, flexibility, and cost (Galinsky, 1988). The one strong exception seems to be those parents who rely on their children to care for themselves or their younger siblings. In a study conducted at Portland State University (Emlen & Koren, 1984), 57% of the sample of more than 8,000 employed parents reported dissatisfaction with latchkey arrangements as compared to 23% using family child care or centers. Taken together, these studies suggest that parents' definition of overall child care satisfaction is primarily influenced by their view of the nature of the child's experience. Parents may be dissatisfied with aspects that affect them, but as long as they feel the child's experience is satisfactory, they are satisfied with the arrangement.

One of the disturbing findings of the Parent/Teacher Study was that parents were quite satisfied with programs deemed low in quality by independent researchers. Parents were more attuned to quality when their children were preschoolers as opposed to infants and toddlers. Unfortunately, parents were more satisfied when there were more children per adult and group sizes were larger. Parents, however, did respond to the quality of the relationship between their child and the teacher-caregiver. When these adults were judged to be more detached, insensitive, or chaotic, parents were less satisfied, lonelier, and missed their child more (Galinsky, Shinn, Phillips, Howes, & Whitebook, 1990). Thus, it seems that while parents are aware of the importance of the teacher-child relationship, they do not

Parents' definition of overall satisfaction with child care is primarily influenced by the nature of their child's experience.

know that having fewer children per adult, smaller group sizes, and adequate preparation of the staff make it more likely that the teacher-caregiver will be nurturing and caring as well as able to teach in developmentally appropriate ways.

Parents in this study were very aware of the amount of staff turnover in the center. When the turnover was higher, parents were less satisfied with the program and were less likely to feel that their child benefitted from the experience. These parents also felt less adequate as parents and missed their children more while at work.

When early childhood professionals assess quality, they find a selection process at work that disadvantages the most at-risk parents. For example, Carollee Howes (Howes & Stewart, 1987) found that families who were under the most stress enrolled their children in the lowest quality child care arrangements. This finding led the National Academy of Sciences Panel on Child Care to conclude that such children are in double jeopardy, experiencing stress from their homes and from poorer child care arrangements (Hayes, Palmer, & Zaslow, 1990).

Often the reasons for selecting poorer quality arrangements are economic (Culkin, Helburn, Morris, & Watson, 1990). Sometimes, however, the results may be surprising. For example, the National Child Care Staffing Study (Whitebook et al., 1990) found that children from low-income families were much more likely to be enrolled in nonprofit programs, and children from higher income families were somewhat more likely to be enrolled in nonprofit programs. Children from middle-income families were much more likely to be enrolled in for-profit programs. In this study, auspice (nonprofit or for-profit) was the strongest predictor of quality. As a result, children from middle-income families were found to be enrolled in centers of lower quality than children from either low- or high-income families.

A patchwork system

Our studies show that parents do not use one arrangement for each child; they piece together a patchwork system. In a study we conducted several years ago, parents at Merck & Co., Inc. reported an average of 1.7 arrangements per child (Galinsky, 1988). A study by Marybeth Shinn and her colleagues (Shinn, Ortiz-Torres, Morris, Simko, & Wong, 1989) from New York University also came up with the same number—1.7. In the *Fortune* magazine study (Galinsky & Hughes, 1987), we found that 38% of the families had to contend with as many as three to four different child care arrangements.

The more arrangements the family has, the more likely they are to fall apart. The issue of child care breakdowns is of great concern because of the high turnover in child care. In the *Fortune* magazine study (Galinsky & Hughes, 1987), we found that 27% of the employed fathers and 24% of the employed mothers had been forced to make two to five special arrangements in the past 3 months because their regular arrangements had fallen apart.

Often the reasons for selecting poorer quality arrangements are economic.

Child care breakdowns are strongly associated with productivity. According to Shinn and her colleagues (Shinn et al., 1989), parents with more breakdowns are more likely to miss work. In the *Fortune* magazine study (Galinsky & Hughes, 1987), we found such parents more likely to come to work late or leave early. In fact, in that study, 72% of all employee tardiness was for family-related reasons.

Parents who face more frequent breakdowns in their child care arrangements report spending more unproductive time at work, according to the *Fortune* magazine study. A study conducted of two New England companies (Burden & Googins, 1987), found that one of every four employed parents said that they worried about their children "always" or "most of the time" while on the job. Such intense reactions to child care problems are expressed by an inability to concentrate on the job and a loss of productivity.

Our research also reveals links between child care breakdown and stress, including stress-related health problems. Parents who had to make more last minute arrangements were more likely to report such symptoms as pains in the back, head, and neck; shortness of breath; heart pounding or racing; as well as eating, drinking, or smoking more than usual (Galinsky, 1988).

It is evident that parents who cannot find quality care, who piece together multiple and tenuous arrangements, who have latchkey children, and who face frequent breakdowns in their child care systems have poorer work attendance, are less able to concentrate on the job, and have more stress-related health problems. Thus, as a nation we are paying the cost of these parents' diminished job performance right now.

THE EFFECT OF QUALITY ON TEACHER-CAREGIVERS

When we think of the impact of quality child care arrangements, we think of children or perhaps their parents, but seldom of the adults who provide care and education to young children. Although there has been a great deal of research on the working conditions of employees in most fields, there has been a notable absence of such research in the early childhood field until very recently. Perhaps this is related to the common assumption that early childhood teacher-caregivers are motivated by their love and concern for young children, so working conditions don't seem so important.

The staffing shortages that face so many early childhood programs across the country are calling this assumption into question. It has become evident that teacher-caregivers of young children can no longer afford to stay in such a low-paying field and are having to leave their jobs. Consequently, studies are beginning to be done to identify the various predictors of job satisfaction and turnover.

Parents who face more frequent breakdowns in their child care arrangements report spending more unproductive time at work.

Job satisfaction

Paula Jorde-Bloom's research (1988) has related various job conditions to the job satisfaction of those working with young children. Among the most salient are job autonomy, relationships with one's supervisor and co-workers, and job clarity. Several studies have found that working in early childhood programs often provides high levels of satisfaction among these variables. For example, teachers in the National Child Care Staffing Study (Whitebook et al., 1990) reported very high levels of satisfaction with the daily demands of their work. In an Indiana study, Susan Kontos and Andrew Stremmel (1988) found that the majority of child care teachers enjoy their work and want to stay in the field. Likewise, in a study of publicly funded programs in New York City, Bob Granger and Elisabeth Marx (1988) found high levels of job satisfaction among such aspects as working with children, intellectual challenge, and opportunities for creativity.

Salaries and benefits

While the high levels of intrinsic measures of job satisfaction reported by child care teachers are important, they cannot overcome the harsh realities of inadequate compensation. In a California study by Michael Olenick (1986), staff retention was higher in programs that paid higher wages. These not unexpected findings were confirmed by the National Child Care Staffing Study (Whitebook et al., 1990). Teachers' wages were the most important predictor of turnover, reported on average at 41% annually. This study found an important relationship between salaries and program quality. Programs that met recognized measures of higher quality also paid better wages and provided more benefits. Staff in these programs reported higher levels of job satisfaction and were more sensitive, less harsh, and engaged in more appropriate caregiving with children.

Similar findings were evident in the Granger and Marx study (1988). Teachers in publicly funded child care and Head Start programs scored significantly lower on several measures of job stability (total years taught, years at current site, and years in current system) than teachers of preschool children in the public school. Demonstrating the relationship between stability and compensation, teachers in programs funded by the public schools received average annual salaries of over $33,000, while those in publicly funded child care and Head Start received annual salaries of just over $19,000. Only a small amount of the disparity was due to differences in education and experience. Granger and Marx estimated that if teachers in the publicly funded child care and Head Start programs were paid according to public school salary schedules, their salaries would have been approximately $31,000 and $27,000 respectively.

In subsequent research, Marx, Zinsser, and Porter (1990) analyzed the impact of 1988 state legislation in New York enacting a one-time child care salary enhancement. Before this legislation was implemented, turnover rates exceeded 30% for teachers and reached 57%

The high level of intrinsic job satisfaction in working with young children is important, but cannot overcome the harsh realities of inadequate compensation.

for aides and assistants in upstate New York. The $12 million enhancement reached 10,270 full-time equivalent staff, each receiving just over $1,200 on average. Turnover was reduced considerably as a result. In New York City, for example, classroom teachers and supervisory staff had a turnover rate of 42% before enactment. A year following the bill's passage, turnover had dropped to 22%. Staff vacancy rates were also cut in half. Thus, not only are poor salaries linked to higher turnover, but also improved salaries lead to reduced turnover.

When early childhood teacher-caregivers broach the issue of inadequate salaries, it can sound self-serving—professionals trying to aggrandize themselves. Considering the below poverty level wages of those working in most child care and early education programs and the subsequent high rates of staff turnover, the issue must be seen as one of quality. In order to provide quality for children, the early childhood field must be able to attract and retain qualified staff. As described throughout this chapter, children and their families are paying the costs of the lack of quality that results from an insufficient pool of qualified staff.

WHAT CAN BE DONE

Slowly but surely, families and organizations within both the public and private sectors are recognizing that the costs of not providing quality early childhood programs are too high to pay. For example, much time and energy has been devoted to the successful passage of federal child care legislation, accomplished in the fall of 1990 after more than 20 years of effort. A number of promising approaches are also occurring at state and local levels. In addition, there are many private sector initiatives which demonstrate growing understanding of need to address quality.

While the specifics of these different efforts vary, some general principles can be applied to the efforts that show the most promise. As the chapters in this volume describe, there is a complex interplay between quality, affordability, and accessibility. Efforts must be considered in light of their effects on each of these variables.

First and foremost, efforts should be built on the idea that parents must have a choice in selecting the program option that best meets their needs. In order to provide parents with meaningful choices, it is necessary to increase and fortify the existing system of community programs. Issues of supply may be addressed by providing start-up loans or grants to potential programs or providing loans or grants for program expansion. Real choice also depends on parents being able to afford good programs. Low- and moderate-income families especially need assistance to afford the full costs of quality programs, not dependent on the hidden subsidy of inadequate staff compensation.

Efforts are needed to improve the quality of existing services. Improved regulatory standards—and effective enforcement—are es-

The costs of not providing quality early childhood programs are too high to pay.

sential. State licensing standards should safeguard the protection of children in settings outside their home and promote their development. In many states, current standards do not afford basic protection to children. In other states, rapid growth in the number of programs has outpaced the number of licensing officials. State budgetary cutbacks have in some instances led to fewer licensing officials in spite of the tremendous growth in the total number of centers and family child care homes subject to regulation.

In addition to regulatory approaches, quality can be enhanced by assisting programs and their staff to participate in professional systems of improvement and recognition. Public/private partnerships have been established to assist programs in achieving accreditation by NAEYC's Academy for centers or the National Family Day Care Association for family child care providers. Assistance may also be provided for individuals to gain professional training and credentials such as the Child Development Associate Credential, administered by the Council for Early Childhood Professional Recognition.

No one segment of our society can solve this nation's child care crisis—not the federal government, not states, not employers, and certainly not families. Instead, all segments of society must join together. The federal government must work as a partner with state and local government, business, religious groups, and social service and philanthropic organizations. Years of research knowledge about the ingredients and effects of quality make it evident that we are losing a great deal by not responding to the crisis of inadequate, tenuous, and poor quality care and education for our nation's youngest citizens. If we don't respond now, we will pay even more for our negligence in the future.

REFERENCES

Adams, G. (1990). *Who knows how safe? The status of state efforts to ensure quality child care.* Washington, DC: Children's Defense Fund.

Aronson, S. (1987). Maintaining health in child care settings. In B.M. Caldwell (Ed.), *Group care for young children: A supplement to parental care.* Proceedings of the 12th Johnson & Johnson Pediatric Round Table (pp. 163–172). Lexington, MA: Lexington Books.

Bredekamp, S. (1989). *Regulating child care quality: Evidence from NAEYC's accreditation system.* Washington, DC: NAEYC.

Burden, D., & Googins, B. (1987, August). *Boston University—Balancing Job and Homelife Study: Summary of results.* Paper presented at the Annual Convention of the American Psychological Association, New York, NY.

Copple, C.E., Cline, M.G., & Smith, A.N. (1987). *Path to the future: Long-term effects of Head Start in the Philadelphia School District.* Washington, DC: U.S. Department of Health and Human Services.

Culkin, M., Helburn, S., Morris, J., & Watson, B. (1990). *Colorado's children: An economic profile of early childhood care and education.* Denver: University of Colorado at Denver, Economics Department.

No one segment of society can solve this nation's child care crisis; all segments of society must join together.

Cummings, E.M. (1986, April). *Caregiver stability in day care: Continuity vs. daily association.* Paper presented at the International Conference on Infant Studies, Los Angeles.

Elkind, D. (1987). *Miseducation: Preschoolers at risk.* New York: Alfred A. Knopf.

Emlen, A., & Koren, P. (1984). *Hard to find and difficult to manage: The effects of child care on the workplace.* Portland, OR: Regional Institute for Human Services.

Finkelstein, N.W. (1982). Aggression: Is it stimulated by day care? *Young Children,* 37(6), 3-9.

Galinsky, E. (1988, January). *The impact of child care problems on parents on the job and at home.* Paper presented at the Wingspread Conference of Child Care Action Campaign, Racine, WI.

Galinsky, E., & Hughes, D. (1987, August). *The Fortune Magazine child care study.* Paper presented at the Annual Convention of the American Psychological Association, New York, NY.

Galinsky, E., Shinn, M., Phillips, D., Howes, C., & Whitebook, M. (1990). *Parent/ teacher relationships.* New York: Families and Work Institute.

Gamble, T.J., & Zigler, E. (1986). Effects of infant day care: Another look at the evidence. *American Journal of Orthopsychiatry,* 56(1), 26-42.

Granger, R.C., & Marx, E. (1988). *Who is teaching? Early childhood teachers in New York City's publicly funded programs.* New York: Bank Street College of Education.

Hayes, C.D., Palmer, J.L., & Zaslow, M.J. (1990). *Who cares for America's children? Child care policy for the 1990s.* Washington, DC: National Academy of Sciences Press.

Howes, C. (1990) Can the age of entry into child care and the quality of child care predict behaviors in kindergarten? *Developmental Psychology,* 26(2), 292-303.

Howes, C., Rodning, C., Galluzzo, D.C., & Myers, L. (1988). Attachment and child care: Relationships with mother and caregiver. *Early Childhood Research Quarterly,* 3(4), 403-416.

Howes, C., & Stewart, P. (1987). Child's play with adults, toys, and peers: An examination of family and child care influences. *Developmental Psychology,* 23(3), 423-430.

Jorde-Bloom, P. (1988). *A great place to work: Improving conditions for staff in young children's programs.* Washington, DC: NAEYC.

Kontos, S., & Stremmel, A.J. (1988). Caregivers' perceptions of working conditions in a child care environment. *Early Childhood Research Quarterly,* 3(1), 77-90.

Lally, J.R., Mangione, P.L., & Honig, A.S. (1987). The Syracuse University Family Development Research Program: Long range impact of early intervention on low-income children and their families. San Francisco: Center for Child & Family Studies, Far West Laboratory for Educational Research and Development. [Summary appears in *Zero to Three,* April, 1988, as "More pride, less delinquency: Findings from the ten-year follow-up of the Syracuse Family Development Research Program," newsletter published by the National Center for Clinical Infant Programs, Arlington, VA.]

Marx, E., & Zinsser, C., with T. Porter. (1990). *Raising child care salaries and benefits: An evaluation of the New York state salary enhancement legislation.* New York: Bank Street College and the Center for Public Advocacy Research.

McCartney, K. (1984). The effect of quality on the day care environment upon children's language development. *Developmental Psychology,* 20, 244-260.

National Council of Jewish Women (1988). [Mothers in the workplace]. Unpublished raw data.

Olenick, M. (1986). *The relationship between day care quality and selected social policy variables.* Dissertation submitted to the UCLA School of Education.

Phillips, D.A., & Howes, C. (1987). Indicators of quality in child care: Review of research. In D.A. Phillips (Ed.), *Quality in child care: What does research tell us?* Washington, DC: NAEYC.

Phillips, D., McCartney, K., & Scarr, S. (1987). Child care quality and children's social development. *Developmental Psychology, 23,* 537-543.

Ruopp, R., Travers, J., Glantz, F., & Coelen, C. (1979). *Children at the center: Final report of the National Day Care Study.* Cambridge, MA: Abt Associates.

Shinn, M., Galinsky, E., & Gulcur, L. (1990). The role of child care centers in the lives of parents. New York: Families and Work Institute.

Shinn, M., Galinsky, E., & Gulcur, L. (1990). [The parent/teacher study.] unpublished raw data.

Shinn, M., Ortiz-Torres, B., Morris, A., Simko, P., & Wong, N. (1989). Promoting the well-being of working parents: Coping, social support, and flexible job schedules. *American Journal of Community Psychology, 17,* 31-55.

Vandell, D.L., Henderson, V.K., & Wilson, K.S. (1988). A longitudinal study of children with varying day care experiences. *Child Development, 59,* 1286-1292.

Vandell, D.L., & Powers, C.P. (1983). Daycare quality and children's free play activities. *American Journal of Orthopsychiatry, 53*(3), 493-500.

Weikart, D.P. (1990, February 26). Testimony at the Subcommittee on Education and Health, Joint Economic Committee, U.S. Congress, Washington, DC.

Whitebook, M., Howes, C., & Phillips, D. (1990). *Who cares? Child care teachers and the quality of care in America. Final report of the National Child Care Staffing Study.* Oakland, CA: Child Care Employee Project.

An Overview of NAEYC's Criteria for High Quality in Early Childhood Programs

4

Sue Bredekamp

NAEYC's ACCREDITATION SYSTEM provides a mechanism for early childhood programs to evaluate and improve their services. It also offers consumers a means of identifying high quality centers serving young children birth through age 5 and school-age children before and after school. Administered by the National Academy of Early Childhood Programs, a division of NAEYC, the system is the only professionally sponsored, national, voluntary accreditation process for all types of early childhood centers and schools. The Criteria for high quality, summarized here, provide the basis for the accreditation process. The Criteria represent the current consensus of the early childhood profession regarding the definition of a high quality program for young children. The Criteria were developed over a 4-year period, drawing upon the knowledge and practical experience of thousands of early childhood educators throughout the country. The Criteria serve as a standard of excellence for any group program. Following the adoption of the Criteria, NAEYC adopted a position statement defining developmentally appropriate practice, extending the definitions for quality to include programs serving children in the primary grades of school.

The Criteria address all aspects of program provision, focusing on ten broad components. These include interactions among staff and children, curriculum, staff-parent interactions, staff qualifications and development, administration, staffing, physical environment, health and safety, nutrition and food service, and evaluation. The following section summarizes each of these areas and provides concrete indicators of each of the major elements of quality, based on the Academy Criteria. Specific examples follow each indicator. For further information, readers are referred to *Accreditation Criteria and Procedures of the National Academy of Early Childhood Programs* (NAEYC #920) and *Developmentally Appropriate Practice in Early Childhood Programs Serving Children Birth through Age 8* (NAEYC # 224).

The Criteria serve as a standard of excellence for any group program.

STAFF-CHILD INTERACTION

Interactions between children and staff provide opportunities for children to develop an understanding of self and others and are characterized by warmth, personal respect, individuality, and responsiveness. Staff facilitate interactions among children to provide opportunities for development of social skills and intellectual growth.

- **Conversation**

    Adults spend the major share of their time talking to, listening to, and closely observing the children. Adults engage children in conversation, at their eye level, that encourages them to express their feelings and ideas.

- **Activity**

    The environment is primarily marked by pleasant conversation, spontaneous laughter, and exclamations of excitement rather than harsh, stressful noise or enforced quiet.

- **Involved children**

    Children and adults are actively involved with each other and with materials. Adults help children play cooperatively. Aimless wandering, fighting, and withdrawn behavior is kept to a minimum.

- **Accessible teachers**

    Children show no hesitation to approach adults with questions, bids for affection, and requests for help. Adults liberally provide individual attention when they are asked or when it is needed. Adults do not spend long periods talking to other adults or involved in housekeeping chores that don't include children.

- **Affection**

    Affection is expressed spontaneously and frequently, and children in distress are comforted.

CURRICULUM

The curriculum, or educational plan, encourages children to be actively involved in the learning process, to experience a variety of activities appropriate to their age and rate of development, and to pursue their own interests in the context of life in the community and the world. Children learn through play that is organized by adults to teach them language, concepts about the physical world, social skills, problem solving, motor coordination, and self-confidence.

- **Variety**

  A wide variety of materials is available, geared to young children's interests, such as picture books, records, puppets, blocks, puzzles, paints, climbing equipment, and props for make-believe play.

- **Involvement**

  Hands-on activity is encouraged. Materials are readily accessible to the children, for example, toys are on low shelves, not in toy boxes. Children are busy and actively involved with the materials, rather than passively watching or following rote instructions.

- **Child-initiated activities**

  The planned, daily schedule balances indoor and outdoor activities, quiet time and active time, periods when individual children choose their own activities and periods for group activities, and child-initiated and adult-initiated activities.

- **Teacher-guided activities**

  The teachers' role is to plan and arrange the learning environment. It is important to see adults asking questions of children, reading

EARLY CHILDHOOD PROGRAM ACCREDITATION— A COMMITMENT TO EXCELLENCE

The National Academy of Early Childhood Programs is an independent accrediting system sponsored by NAEYC. Early childhood program accreditation means that

- An early childhood program—child care center, preschool, kindergarten, or before- and/or after-school program—**voluntarily applied** for accreditation by the National Academy of Early Childhood Programs.

- The program then engaged in an **extensive self-study** based on the Academy's Criteria for High Quality Early Childhood Programs.

- The accuracy of the program's self-study was **verified during a site visit** to the program by a team of trained volunteer validators.

- The validated self-study, including the program director's responses to the validation visit, was **reviewed by a 3-member national commission** composed of recognized experts in child care and early childhood education.

- Accredited programs are judged to be **in substantial compliance** with the Academy's Criteria and **granted accreditation** for a three-year period.

- The early childhood program **agreed to act upon the Commission's suggestions** regarding areas of marginal compliance with the Criteria and to submit annual written reports documenting improvements and continued compliance.

to children, making suggestions, challenging and extending children's thinking, setting up new experiences such as a special visitor or holiday celebration, adding new materials as children master familiar tasks, and observing and recording children's progress in acquiring new skills and interests.

- **Cultural diversity**

  Multi-racial, multicultural, nonsexist, nonstereotyping pictures, dolls, books, and materials are fully part of the classroom to teach children the value of diversity and to ensure that all children's backgrounds are respected.

- **Responsibilities**

  Daily, routine activities are part of the learning process. For example, children are given responsibility for setting tables at mealtime and helping with clean-up during the day.

COMMUNICATION WITH PARENTS

All communication between centers and families is based on the concept that parents are the principal influence in children's lives. Parents are well-informed about and welcome as observers and contributors to the program.

- **Informed parents**

  Parents are given written information about what to expect from the program and what the program expects from them through a parent handbook, newsletters, bulletin boards, and other similar measures.

- **Home-school communication**

  Parents have opportunities to communicate with the staff about their individual child's needs and progress through notes, phone calls, conferences, and face-to-face conversations at arrival and pick-up.

- **Welcome access**

  Parents are welcome in the center at all times and are encouraged to participate in a variety of ways, such as eating lunch with the children, observing during the day, volunteering to help, and attending parent meetings.

STAFF HIRING AND QUALIFICATIONS

The quality and competence of the staff are the most important determinants of the quality of an early childhood program and of

positive outcomes for children. It is critical, therefore, that the program is staffed by adults who are trained in child development and early education and who recognize and provide for children's needs.

• **Careful hiring**

Hiring procedures include careful checking of personal references of all potential new employees. New staff members serve a probationary employment period during which the director makes a professional judgment of their suitability for working with children.

• **Trained teachers**

Entry requirements for directors and teachers include training in early childhood education and child development. The training must include specific instruction in the age groups for which the adult is responsible. The amount of training required varies with the level of professional responsibility of the position. The director has also received training or has experience in program administration.

• **In-service training**

The program provides regular in-service training for staff to improve and expand skills in working with children and their families.

• **Record keeping**

Accurate and current records are kept of staff qualifications, including transcripts, letters of reference, and documentation of in-service education.

STAFFING STRUCTURE

The program is sufficiently staffed and organized to assure that the needs of individual children are met, and to maintain positive interactions and constructive activity among the children and staff.

• **Supervision**

There is a sufficient number of adults for the number of children in the program to ensure adequate supervision, frequent personal contact, and time for individual instruction as needed. Recommendations vary by age, ranging from 3 infants per adult to 10 to 12 school-age children per adult.

• **Continuity**

Staffing patterns are planned so that the same adults have primary responsibility for the same children each day. This allows for

NAEYC ACCREDITATION CRITERIA
RECOMMENDED STAFF-CHILD RATIOS WITHIN GROUP SIZE

					Size of Group						
Age of children	6	8	10	12	14	16	18	20	22	24	28
Infants (birth–12 mos.)	1:3	1:4									
Toddlers (12–24 mos.)	1:3	1:4	1:5	1:4							
Two-year-olds (24–30 mos.)		1:4	1:5	1:6							
Two-1/2-years (30–36 mos.)				1:6	1:7						
Three-year-olds					1:7	1:8	1:9	1:10			
Four-year-olds						1:8	1:9	1:10			
Five-year-olds						1:8	1:9	1:10			
Six- to eight-year-olds								1:10	1:11	1:12	
Nine- to twelve-year-olds										1:12	1:14

Smaller group sizes and lower staff-child ratios have been found to be strong predictors of compliance with indicators of quality such as positive interactions among staff and children and developmentally appropriate curriculum. Variations in group sizes and ratios are acceptable only in cases where the program demonstrates a very high level of compliance with criteria for interactions, curriculum, staff qualifications, health and safety, and physical environment.

greater consistency in the daily experiences of children and enables the staff to be highly familiar with the child's needs, interests, and background.

- **Small groups**

The number of children in a group is limited to facilitate constructive interaction and activity. For infants, groups should not exceed 6 to 8 children. Group size will increase with age, but should not exceed 20 for older preschool children and 28 for school-age children.

PROGRAM ADMINISTRATION

The quality of the early childhood experience for children is affected by the efficiency and stability of the program's administration. Effective administration includes good communication, positive community relations, fiscal stability, and attention to the needs and working conditions of staff members.

- **Written policies and procedures**

The program has written policies and operating procedures.

- **Record keeping**

  Program records, such as attendance, health, budgets, board meetings, and confidential personnel files are maintained and regularly updated.

- **Insurance**

  Accident protection and liability insurance coverage is maintained for children and adults.

- **Staff meetings**

  Staff meetings are held regularly to facilitate joint planning.

- **Self-evaluation**

  At least annually, the educational plan and fiscal records are assessed to identify program strengths and weaknesses and to specify program goals for the year.

PHYSICAL ENVIRONMENT

The indoor and outdoor physical environments should be designed to promote involvement in the daily activities and easy, constructive interactions among adults and children.

- **Space**

  The amount of space is adequate so children are not crowded and freedom of movement is encouraged.

- **Easy movement**

  The room arrangement and placement of materials make it easy to identify different activity areas (block building, book corner, water play, dress-up areas, for example) and to move from one area to another. Views are not obstructed so adults can easily observe the children.

- **Activity areas**

  Indoor space is arranged to provide a variety of activities. For example, there are areas for children to work individually, together in small groups or in a large group. There is space for both active and quiet activities.

- **Exercise**

  Outdoor space and equipment also allow a variety of activities, such as riding, climbing, balancing, sand play and digging, and individual play. The outdoor area includes a variety of surfaces such as soil, sand, grass, hills, flat sections, and hard surfaces for wheel toys.

HEALTH AND SAFETY

The health and safety of children and adults are protected and enhanced. Good programs act to prevent illness and accidents, are prepared to deal with emergencies should they occur, and also educate children concerning safe and healthy practices.

- **Licensed program**

  The program is licensed, and therefore is in compliance with legal requirements for the health and safety of children in group settings.

- **Health records**

  Health records, including immunization records and emergency contact information, are complete and available for each child.

- **Maintenance**

  The building and equipment are maintained in safe, clean condition and in good repair.

- **Supervision**

  Children are supervised by adults at all times and are released only to authorized persons.

- **Transportation safety**

  If transportation is provided for children, vehicles are equipped with age-appropriate restraint devices.

- **Accident reporting**

  All medical problems and accidents are recorded and reported to staff and parents. Suspected incidents of child abuse by parents, staff, or others are reported to appropriate local agencies.

- **Emergency procedures**

  Written emergency procedures are posted, and staff are familiar with these procedures and with evacuation routes.

- **Handwashing**

  Staff wash their hands before feeding and after diapering. Children wash their hands after toileting and before meals.

- **Safe equipment**

  Cushioning materials such as mats, wood chips, or sand are used under climbers, slides, and swings. Equipment of this type is securely anchored.

- **Product safety**

  All potentially dangerous products such as medicines or cleaning supplies are stored in original, labeled containers in locked cabinets inaccessible to children.

NUTRITION AND FOOD SERVICE

Children are provided with adequate nutrition and are educated concerning good eating habits.

- **Well-balanced meals**

  Well-balanced meals and snacks meet the child's nutritional requirements as determined by the amount of time the child spends in the program.

- **Social interaction**

  Mealtimes are pleasant social and learning experiences for children. For example, children serve and feed themselves as their age permits, eating utensils and portions are child-sized, and conversation is encouraged.

- **Sound nutritional practices**

  Food preparation and storage is in compliance with legal requirements.

EVALUATION

Ongoing and systematic evaluation is essential to improving and maintaining the quality of an early childhood program. Evaluation should focus on the program's effectiveness in meeting the needs of children and parents.

- **Staff evaluations**

  Evaluations should provide for self-assessment and classroom observation by the director or other appropriate person, with opportunities for private discussion and feedback.

- **Records of children's development**

  Individual descriptions of children's development should be written and compiled, forming the basis for communication with parents and planning optimal learning activities.

- **Participation by all interested parties**

  Parents, staff, and other professionals should have at least an annual opportunity to evaluate the program's effectiveness.

NAEYC Position Statement on Guidelines for Compensation of Early Childhood Professionals

5

Adopted July 1990

GIVEN THE IMPORTANCE of the early childhood years in shaping later development and learning and the increasing number of families relying on early childhood programs, it is crucial that such programs employ personnel with the knowledge and ability needed to provide good care and education for our nation's youngest citizens. While the need to provide additional public and private support to improve affordability and quality of early childhood services has gained better understanding in recent years, more remains to be done. NAEYC calls for all sectors of society to further their efforts to improve the affordability and quality of early childhood services. If children are to receive the level of care and education they deserve, these efforts must rectify the inadequate compensation of program staff.

NAEYC recommends that the following guidelines be used in decisions related to the provision of compensation of early childhood professionals. It is recognized that some early childhood programs will require additional resources before these guidelines can be implemented. Families alone cannot be expected to bear the additional costs. NAEYC is committed to working for strategies that acknowledge the full cost of quality early childhood program provision and that distribute these costs more equitably among all sectors of society. NAEYC believes that parents and early childhood professionals have borne a disproportionate burden in the provision of early childhood programs. All of society—children, families, employers, communities, and the nation as a whole—benefits from the provision of high quality early childhood programs. It is time that the full cost of this essential public service be shared more equitably by all sectors of society.

- **Early childhood professionals with comparable qualifications, experience, and job responsibilities should receive comparable compensation regardless of the setting of their job. This means that a teacher working in a community child care center, a family child care provider, and an elementary school teacher who each hold comparable professional qualifications should also receive comparable compensation for their work.**

Early childhood professionals who work directly with young children typically are employed in a variety of settings including public schools; part-day and full-day centers, whether for-profit or non-profit; public and private prekindergarten programs, including Head Start; before- and after-school programs; and family child care. Despite the differences in setting, the nature of the job responsibilities are generally similar.

While the work of all early childhood professionals has been under-valued, those professionals working with children in situations other than serving school-age children during the traditional school-day have been the most undercompensated. For example, a recent national study (U.S. General Accounting Office, 1989) found that teachers in early childhood programs accredited by NAEYC earned roughly half their counterparts in public schools, holding education and experience constant. Even within the public school, salaries have been found to be depressed for equally qualified teachers of preschool children, especially when program funding is based on parent fees or special program subsidies (Mitchell & Modigliani, 1989). As a matter of equity, early childhood professionals who have comparable qualifications and job responsibilities should also receive comparable compensation.

- **Compensation for early childhood professionals should be equivalent to that of other professionals with comparable preparation requirements, experience, and job responsibilities.**

While removing disparity within the early childhood profession is an important step forward, given the under-valuing of all work with young children, it is an insufficient goal. Early childhood salary schedules and benefits should be determined following a review of salary schedules for members of other professional groups. Reviews should be conducted within the community and when feasible, within the early childhood program's larger organizational structure.

Although an institutional review may not be feasible for small independent programs, it has proven to be an effective tool for improving compensation in many programs associated with a larger institution. The institutional review is an internal review, considering salaries and benefits provided to individuals with similar preparation and responsibilities. For example, a community service organization may compare the salaries and benefits of its early childhood teaching staff to its social workers with equivalent preparation and responsibility. A public school would examine the comparability of responsibilities and preparation and corresponding compensation for teachers in its prekindergarten and kindergarten programs to secondary teachers. The compensation of a program administrator in an organization such as a hospital, industry, or educational institution would be compared to the compensation package of heads of other programs or departments of similar size within that institution.

The community review, possible for all programs, should begin by considering professionals with similar responsibilities. The job responsibilities of early childhood professionals are most comparable to those of other educational professionals in elementary and secondary schools. The community review should also take into account other professionals in the community. These may include nurses, social workers, and counselors as well as others. Many of the social services share with the early childhood profession in the undervaluing of their work; broader comparability to more equitably paid professions should be the long-term goal.

It should be noted that family child care providers are typically not salaried employees, but are self-employed with income based on fees for service. Community reviews may provide useful information for family child care providers when determining fees. Fees should be based on the full cost of providing a high quality service and include sufficient compensation for the level of professional preparation.

- **Compensation should not be differentiated on the basis of the ages of children served.**

Assuming equivalent professional preparation and equivalent job responsibilities, early childhood professionals working with young children should receive compensation comparable to professionals working with older children. Typically, the younger the child, the less the value placed on the service provided. Yet, children are most vulnerable in their early years, and the impact of their early experiences on later development and learning is the most profound. Compensation provided to individuals working with young children should reflect the importance of their work.

- **Early childhood professionals should be encouraged to seek additional professional preparation and should be rewarded accordingly.**

Currently there is little incentive for early childhood personnel to seek additional training. Despite the lack of public understanding as to its importance, specialized knowledge of how young children develop and learn is the key predictor of how well early childhood personnel are able to implement a developmentally appropriate program (Bredekamp, 1989). Even when individuals understand the importance of professional development for improving the quality of early childhood services, access to continuing education is often denied due to a lack of resources.

The current crisis in recruiting and retaining qualified staff has resulted in many programs employing individuals who are underqualified for their roles and responsibilities. The provision of inservice training is especially critical in these situations so that children receive the quality of care they need. When the acquisition of additional preparation is not rewarded, there is little incentive for these individuals to remain on the job and the investment made in their inservice training is lost.

• **The provision of an adequate benefits package is a crucial component of compensation for early childhood staff.**

Early childhood personnel who are satisfied with their jobs and whose individual and family members' health is protected are more likely to convey positive feelings toward children, are more able to give utmost attention to teaching and caring for children, and are more likely to remain in their positions for longer periods of time. Benefits packages for full-time staff may be negotiated to meet individual staff members' needs but should include paid leave (annual, sick, and/or personal), medical insurance, and retirement and may provide educational benefits, subsidized child care, or other options unique to the situation. Benefits for part-time staff should be provided on a pro-rated basis. (Students or others who are placed on the job on a temporary basis for job-training purposes are excluded from this provision.)

• **A career ladder should be established, providing additional increments in salary based on performance and participation in professional development opportunities.**

Individuals who work directly with young children should be able to envision a future in this work. Too often, the only opportunity for advancement in early childhood programs requires leaving direct work with children. A career ladder which offers opportunities for advancement through merit increases and recognition of higher levels of preparation and mastery of practice promotes higher quality services for children.

REFERENCES

Bredekamp, S. (1989). *Regulating child care quality: Evidence from NAEYC's accreditation system.* Washington, DC: NAEYC.

Mitchell, A. & Modigliani, K. (1989). Public policy report. Young children in the public schools? The "only ifs" reconsidered. *Young Children, 44*(6), 56-61.

U.S. General Accounting Office. (1989). *Early childhood education: Information on costs and services at high quality centers.* Washington, DC: Author.

Estimating the Full Cost of Quality

6

Barbara Willer

QUALITY in an early childhood program depends on whether the full costs of providing a quality service can be sustained. The nature of the child's experience—the heart of quality—is constrained by four parameters. These include a program's ability to

1. **Foster good relationships between children and adults** by limiting group size and the number of children per adult, promoting continuity within the program for children, and enhancing staff-parent relationships;

2. Ensure that educational personnel have qualifications reflecting the **specialized preparation** and **knowledge of child development and early education** needed to work effectively with young children and their families;

3. Provide **adequate compensation** (salaries and benefits) to attract and retain a qualified staff; and

4. Establish an **environment that enhances children's ability to learn** in a safe and stimulating setting and **provides good working conditions for adults.**

Program directors, teacher-caregivers, and advocates have long recognized that the factors which promote quality have a price. But, concerns about affordability have pre-empted discussions of the cost for all programs to provide the level of quality that every child deserves. Affordability constrains quality most when it is assumed that families alone are responsible for the costs of early childhood care and education. When it is recognized that all of society has a stake in the quality of services provided to our nation's youngest citizens and hence a responsibility to help foot the bill, more potential resources are available to pay for quality. It is imperative to know the full cost of providing a quality service so that various segments of society—employers, foundations, service organizations, government—can then determine how they can support these costs.

This chapter provides the information and tools needed to estimate the full costs of quality in early childhood programs. Results of two national studies are used to describe how early childhood programs in general are meeting the full cost parameters. These costs may differ considerably for a particular program, since costs vary significantly

Program directors, teacher-caregivers, and advocates have long recognized that the factors which promote quality have a price.

from one region of the country to another and from urban to rural areas. Costs also depend on the ages of the children served, since group size and staffing requirements are more stringent for younger children and require additional personnel. Some programs may already exceed the average cost suggested as the full cost of quality, yet not fully meet the recommendations for high quality. Thus, the second section of the chapter presents information that may be used to estimate current and full costs for an individual program.

Directors, teacher-caregivers, advocates, and others working to help early childhood programs fully reach high quality should find the worksheets and information for individual programs useful. Although most applicable to centers and family child care homes serving children prior to school entry and/or before- and after-school, the material is also relevant to kindergarten and primary programs in elementary schools.

Public schools may use these materials to determine changes—and costs—needed for providing high quality kindergarten and primary school services. Unlike many programs serving preschool children, public schools have not relied so heavily on subsidies provided by foregone staff compensation. For many schools, the barriers to full quality have been in terms of staffing. Typically, large groups of children are assigned to a single adult, often with no specialized knowledge of child development and early education. For such programs to fully meet high quality recommendations, changes will be needed to ensure appropriate group sizes and adult-child ratios and to ensure that teaching and administrative personnel have the recommended professional preparation in early childhood development and education.

NATIONAL ESTIMATES OF REACHING FULL QUALITY

Unlike many programs serving preschool children, public schools have not relied so heavily on subsidies provided by foregone staff compensation.

The National Child Care Staffing Study (Whitebook, Howes, & Phillips, 1990) and the U.S. General Accounting Office (GAO) *Report on Early Childhood Education: What are the Costs of High-Quality Programs?* (1990) provide important national-level data as to how fully early childhood centers are meeting quality recommendations and their expenditures on program provision. The National Child Care Staffing Study (NCCSS) studied the quality of 227 full-day child care centers in five metropolitan areas: Atlanta, Boston, Detroit, Phoenix, and Seattle. The study was not designed to be nationally representative for statistical purposes. However, the sites were purposively identified to reflect the diversity of public regulatory climates across the nation. For each site, a random sample of programs reflected the diversity of centers within the community. The NCCSS provides important information regarding the characteristics of teaching staff and their working environment in child care centers as well as the relationship between these variables and quality for children.

The GAO study of the costs of high-quality early childhood program provision was commissioned by Senator Edward Kennedy in an effort to determine the costs of providing publicly funded, high-quality early childhood programs to all eligible 4-year-olds. The GAO study collected information from 265 full-day, full-year programs accredited by the National Academy of Early Childhood Programs, a division of NAEYC. Accredited programs are a select group of all early childhood programs which have demonstrated substantial compliance with NAEYC's Criteria for High Quality Early Childhood Programs (Bredekamp, 1987). The Criteria represent professional consensus regarding critical ingredients of high early childhood programs.

The table on the following pages compares selected characteristics of centers as reported by the NCCSS and the GAO studies. The characteristics listed here reflect average results; the NCCSS in particular found tremendous variation from site to site. Similarly, the GAO study reported regional cost variation. The centers studied by the NCCSS are indicative of the quality of all early childhood programs in five metropolitan areas, while the centers examined by the GAO are a highly select group. Some findings are similar. Both studies report that on average programs enroll approximately 80 children and employ a teaching staff of 15 (full-time equivalent) individuals. Beyond basic demographics, there are striking differences in quality characteristics. This is not surprising, given that the NCCSS investigators judged the overall average quality of care in centers as "barely adequate," while accredited programs had already documented substantial compliance with NAEYC's Criteria for high quality.

In general, early childhood centers have a long way to go to fully reach high quality recommendations. Accredited programs have already achieved several dimensions of high quality, especially in terms of promoting good relationships between children and adults and providing good environments for learning and working. Educational staff (teachers, assistants, and directors) in accredited programs have significantly higher levels of both formal education and specific preparation in early childhood education than staff in centers generally. However, further professional development is needed by some individuals, even in accredited centers.

Compensation is the area in which both accredited and other programs lag most from the profession's recommendations for quality. Accredited centers offer significantly greater compensation to staff than programs in general, although teachers in accredited centers still earn approximately half the annualized salaries of comparable public school teachers (GAO, 1990).

The chart on program characteristics also presents budget information collected in the GAO and NCCSS studies. Based on total budgets and the number of children enrolled, a rough estimate can be gained regarding the expenditures per child on quality program provision.

Compensation is the area in which both accredited and other programs lag most from the profession's recommendations for quality.

QUALITY CHARACTERISTICS OF EARLY CHILDHOOD CENTERS

	CENTERS IN GENERAL (NCCSS)	ACCREDITED CENTERS (GAO STUDY)
Ratios and Group size **Percent of Groups greatly** *exceeding* **recommended ratios**	Infants – 16% Toddlers – 15% Preschoolers – 4%[1]	0% 0% 0%
Average Group Size and Range reported **Infants** single age mixed age	(Average/Range) 8.5/4–24 9.6/2–15	Recommended group size 6–8
Toddlers single age mixed age	10.9/4–41 17.1/2–49	Recommended group size 10–14
Preschoolers single age mixed age	16.6/4–45 22.1/3–45	Recommended group size 14–20
Percent greatly *exceeding* **recommended group size** **Infants** (more than 10) **Toddlers** (more than 16) **Preschoolers** (more than 20)	11% 5% 11%	0% 0% 0%
Staffing[2] **Percent of groups with one adult present**	90%	13% (meets recommendations when ratios maintained)
Percent of groups with staff overlap	76%	100%
Staff Turnover (annual)	52%	36%
Staff Qualifications **Directors** Baccalaureate degree or more Associate degree Some college High school graduate Less than high school grad Other	42% -- 30% 20% 12% --	88% 3% -- -- -- 9%

[1]*Preschool figure is percent exceeding recommendation by 50%*
[2]*These comparisons are based on an examination of accredited and nonaccredited centers within NCCSS.*
[3]*Salary comparisons based on 40-hr week, 52-wk year.*
[4]*Budget includes in-kind donations of approximately $600 per child.*

	CENTERS IN GENERAL (NCCSS)	ACCREDITED CENTERS (GAO*)
Staff Qualifications, continued		
Teachers		
Baccalaureate degree or more	31%	52%
Some college	44%	38%
High school graduate	21%	8%
Less than High School	26%	--
Other	--	2%
Assistants		
Baccalaureate degree or more	19%	12%
Some college	37%	48%
High school graduate	33%	30%
Less than high school grad	11%	8%
Other	--	2%
Compensation		
Annual Salaries		
Director	$20,488	$24,300
Teachers	$11,600	$14,100
Assistants	$9,700	$10,200
Benefits[2]		
Percent reporting		
Health benefits	20%	64%
Retirement benefits	14%	335%
Paid preparation and education	2%	3%
Paid breaks	38%	71%
Annual days of sick leave	4.4 days	7.9 days
Selected Program Characteristics		
Total budget	$241,084	$384,000[4]
Average number of children enrolled	84	80
Average number of teachers	15	15
Expenditures per child	$2870	$4800[4]
Percent of budget spent on personnel	70%	65%[4]
Percent of personnel budget spent on teaching staff	82%	74%[4]
Percent of budget based on parent fees	77%	70%[4]

Note that expenditures or cost per child does not equal the fee for service. The NCCSS found on average that parent fees represented 77% of the program budget; for accredited programs, parent fees made up 70% of their budget. The average center's budget based on NCCSS data does not include in-kind services and other donations which are reflected in the accredited programs' budget. In-kind contributions averaged $600 per child or $48,000 for a program serving 80 children. In general, according to the NCCSS, centers spend 70% of their budget on personnel costs; accredited centers reported that 65% of the budget was spent on personnel. This difference may appear surprising, given the higher quality of accredited centers; one would expect higher quality to reflect higher personnel costs. This finding is most likely attributable to the fact that the budget figures for accredited programs include substantial in-kind donations.

The table on the opposite page presents a comparison of a typical center budget and an accredited center budget in relation to budgets designed to reach the full cost of quality. The "improved" and "full cost" budgets are specifically designed to address the current barriers to full cost identified in accredited programs by the GAO study. The primary barrier is inadequate staff compensation. The "improved" budget provides for a considerable salary increase for all educational personel (director and teachers) but does not fully achieve wage comparability to similar professionals. A differentiated staffing structure is employed, reflecting varying levels of preparation and responsibilities corresponding to different levels of compensation. The differentiated staffing structure addresses the need for improved professional preparation by rewarding those with higher qualifications with higher salaries.

The "improved" budget also includes a 10% increase in nonpersonnel costs above accredited centers' costs. The rationale for a fairly small increase in nonpersonnel costs is based on the fact that accredited programs have already met most of the recommendations for creating good environments for learning and working and should not incur substantial additional costs in this regard. The "full cost" budget is based on a similar rationale. Salaries for educational personnel are comparable to other professionals with similar education and job responsibilities (see page 70). There is an additional 10% increase above the "improved" level for nonpersonnel costs.

These estimates are based on the average results reported by the NCCSS And GAO studies. The GAO study reported regional differences in the cost per child ranging from $4,500 in the West to $5,600 in the Northeast. The value of in-kind donations ranged from 10% to 15% of the total budget.

These figures may not reflect the costs of early childhood programs which offer a full range of comprehensive services. The GAO study

The cost per child does not necessarily equal the fee for service.

TABLE 2. A COMPARISON OF COST ESTIMATES			
Estimates based on NCCSS data	**Estimates based on GAO study of accredited centers**	**Improved Estimates** (GAO figures plus improved salaries and 10% increase in nonpersonnel)	**Full Cost Estimates** (Improved plus salary increases to comparability and 10% increase in nonpersonnel)
Total Groups = 5 Ages = All	Total Groups = 5 Ages = All	Total Groups = 5 Ages = All	Total Groups = 5 Ages = All
Teaching Staff 1 director @ $20,488 5 teachers @ $9,975 10 assts. @ $8,173	**Teaching Staff** 1 director @ $24,300 5 teachers @ $14,100 10 assts. @ $10,200	**Teaching Staff** 1 director @ $30,000 2 master teachers @ $22,000 3 teachers @ $20,000 5 asst teachers @ $16,000 5 teaching assts @ $13,500	**Teaching Staff** 1 director @ $40,000 2 master teachers @ $33,000 3 teachers @ $29,000 5 asst teachers @ $23,000 5 teaching assts @ $17,500
Total Educational Salaries = $152,088	**Total Educational Salaries = $196,800**	**Total Educational Salaries = $281,500**	**Total Educational Salaries = $395,500**
Total Budget = $241,084	**Total Budget =** $409,148	**Total Budget =** $537,928	**Total Budget =** $707,734
Annual Cost per Child= $2870	**Annual Cost per Child= $4871**	**Annual Cost per Child= $6404**	**Annual Cost per Child= $8425**

All estimates are based on a program serving 84 children. NCCSS teaching salaries are based on a 35-hour work week for 50 weeks per year, as reported by the NCCSS The remaining columns calculate salaries for a 40-hour work week, 52 weeks per year. The total budget for column 1 is the NCCSS average reported center budget. In the other columns, total budget is calculated based on the percentages reported in the GAO study. In column 2, teaching personnel costs are 74% of the total personnel budget, which is 65% of the total budget. In columns 3 and 4, nonpersonnel costs begin with the nonpersonnel costs reported by GAO for accredited centers and adds a 10% increase at both steps.

noted that less than 25% of the programs surveyed offered formal screening for handicapping conditions and health screening, hallmarks of comprehensive service provision. The need to provide comprehensive services depends on the circumstances of the children served and their families' access to needed services. The GAO study reported that of programs reporting expenditures for supplementary services, the average cost per child for one year was $151. This figure most likely underestimates their cost since many programs did not budget supplementary services separately from educational services or staff salaries. Of programs enrolling children with handicapping conditions, 71% reported providing specialized services to meet their needs, including transportation, speech or physical therapy, counseling, special classroom materials and equipment such as wheelchair ramps, specialized teacher training, and additional personnel.

ESTIMATING THE FULL COST OF QUALITY IN AN INDIVIDUAL PROGRAM

Since there may be considerable variation from national averages to specific program costs, this section focuses on estimating costs for an individual program. While specific costs may vary, broad categories remain constant. As indicated by both the GAO and NCCSS data, personnel costs, especially for educational personnel, are the largest component of an early childhood budget. Three of the four parameters for the full cost of quality affect personnel costs. These include the parameters related to promoting a good relationship between adults and children, ensuring qualified personnel, and providing adequate staff compensation. The costs of meeting each of these parameters is considered in turn. Worksheets are included to help estimate the various costs. Sample worksheets appear throughout the chapter; a complete set of blank worksheets may be found in Appendix 2.

Promoting good relationships

Promoting good relationships between adults and children deals not only with fostering good relationships between staff and children, but also between staff and parents, and ultimately parents and children. It is crucial that staff, parents, and children are able to form warm, trusting relationships with one another and to establish and maintain good communication. These relationships can be enhanced by ensuring an adequate number of adults, limiting the number of children in the group, and scheduling staff to promote continuity for children. Not only will these strategies foster the development of close ties between staff and children, they can help to promote good staff-parent relationships. The fewer children for which individual members of the teaching staff are responsible, the easier it is to also form close relationships with family members.

One of the largest current barriers to the formation of good relationships is the extraordinarily high rate of staff turnover in some programs. It is assumed that improved working conditions and compen-

It is crucial that staff, parents, and children are able to form warm, trusting relationships with one another.

sation will stem turnover and thus promote staff continuity over time. Therefore, this discussion focuses on ensuring continuity for children over the course of the day.

Number of staff

A rough estimate of the total number of teaching personnel needed by a center-based program can be calculated based on the number of hours that children are in attendance and the total number of groups. These calculations assume two adults for each group, meeting recommendations for adult-child ratios by limiting the number of children. For example, if children are enrolled for 10 hours, a minimum of 20 staff hours are needed. Additional time is needed to permit staff to take breaks, provide overlap for shift changes, and provide time for set-up and closing before and after children leave. Time must also be provided for planning and preparation. Providing this additional time requires a minimum of three full-time employees (or full-time equivalents) working 8 hours a day per group of children. If programs operate for a longer day or if staff work fewer than 8 hours a day, additional staff will be required to meet time demands beyond direct contact with children.

These same calculations will hold for larger family child care homes with two adults working with children. When there is only one teacher-caregiver, total group size should be reduced by 50%. A regular substitute should be available to allow the provider to take breaks, attend training, and take vacation and sick or emergency leave.

Staff scheduling

Good staffing is more than a matter of numbers. Given the 10 or more hours of daily operation for many early childhood programs, arranging staffing patterns that meet the guidelines for ratio *and* continuity is not easy. Since many children attend programs for more than an 8-hour workday, changes in personnel will be required over the course of the day. Staffing patterns can promote continuity for children by giving a teaching team primary responsibility for a specific group of children. All adults assigned to the group of children are members of the teaching team. The teaching team shares in the planning of the daily program and activities. Care and education are integrated throughout the day, not separated into "school" or "preschool" in the morning and "child care" or "extended day" in the afternoon. Staffing assignments permit overlap in scheduling to allow for effective planning, assessment, and communication about individual children and the program and activities, not only among team members, but also with parents. Policies and practices are designed to enhance a good working relationship among team members and parents. Particular attention is given to promoting team members' effective interpersonal and communication skills for working effectively with each other as well as with members of children's families.

Staffing patterns can promote continuity for children by giving a teaching team primary responsibility for a specific group of children.

NAEYC ACCREDITATION CRITERIA
RECOMMENDED STAFF-CHILD RATIOS WITHIN GROUP SIZE

						Size of Group					
Age of children	**6**	**8**	**10**	**12**	**14**	**16**	**18**	**20**	**22**	**24**	**28**
Infants (birth–12 mos.)	1:3	1:4									
Toddlers (12–24 mos.)	1:3	1:4	1:5	1:4							
Two-year-olds (24–30 mos.)			1:4	1:5	1:6						
Two-1/2-years (30–36 mos.)				1:6	1:7						
Three-year-olds					1:7	1:8	1:9	1:10			
Four-year-olds						1:8	1:9	1:10			
Five-year-olds						1:8	1:9	1:10			
Six- to eight-year-olds								1:10	1:11	1:12	
Nine- to twelve-year-olds										1:12	1:14

Smaller group sizes and lower staff-child ratios have been found to be strong predictors of compliance with indicators of quality such as positive interactions among staff and children and developmentally appropriate curriculum. Variations in group sizes and ratios are acceptable only in cases where the program demonstrates a very high level of compliance with criteria for interactions, curriculum, staff qualifications, health and safety, and physical environment.

The sample staffing worksheet (next page) illustrates a staffing pattern which promotes good relationships between children and adults. The staffing configurations meet NAEYC's recommendations for group size and adult-child ratio and promote continuity for children over the course of the day. Recommendations represent the *highest* not the average number. Average group size and ratio are *lower* than the recommendations due to overlap and the fact that children arrive and depart at different times. **The Staffing Worksheet (#1)** should be completed based on the program's current staffing patterns. Then answer the questions (boxed at left) to determine how well current staffing meets NAEYC's recommendations.

QUESTIONS TO CONSIDER WHEN
DETERMINING STAFFING PATTERNS

1. Are the group sizes and adult-child ratios within NAEYC's recommendations for the ages of children in the group?

2. Do staffing patterns promote continuity? Do the schedules of staff members overlap or are there complete "shift changes" in personnel?

3. Are staff members given primary responsibility for a group of children, allowing deeper attachments to develop?

4. Do infants spend the majority of their time interacting with the same person over the course of the day?

5. Is there time for staff members to take breaks and for staff preparation and planning, while maintaining appropriate ratios and group sizes if children are present.

6. Is there a specific adult responsible for ongoing communication with the child's family?

Questions adapted from NAEYC accreditation criteria.

WORKSHEET #1: STAFFING WORKSHEET

Group: Infants

GROUP NAME: Infants	AM												PM
NUMBER OF CHILDREN ENROLLED EACH HOUR	6:00	7:00	8:00	9:00	10:00	11:00	12:00	1:00	2:00	3:00	4:00	5:00	6:00	7:00
		2	4/5	6	8	8	8	8	8	8	6/5	4	4/2	

TOTAL NUMBER OF CHILDREN IN GROUP: 8

AGE OF MAJORITY OF CHILDREN IN GROUP: 11 mos.

HOURS OF EACH STAFF MEMBER:
Mary (7-3)
Angie (11-7)
Julia (8-12)
Ann (2:30-6:30)

NUMBER OF TEACHERS PRESENT EACH HOUR													
AM													PM
	1	2	2	2	3	2	2	2/3	2	2	2	2/1	

Group: Older Toddlers

GROUP NAME: Older Toddlers	AM												PM
NUMBER OF CHILDREN ENROLLED EACH HOUR	6:00	7:00	8:00	9:00	10:00	11:00	12:00	1:00	2:00	3:00	4:00	5:00	6:00	7:00
		2	4/7	12	12	12	12	12	12	12	10/8	8/6	3	

TOTAL NUMBER OF CHILDREN IN GROUP: 12

AGE OF MAJORITY OF CHILDREN IN GROUP: 20 mos.

HOURS OF EACH STAFF MEMBER:
Sarah (7-3)
Carol (11-7)
Lou 8-12
Kay (2:30-6:30)

NUMBER OF TEACHERS PRESENT EACH HOUR													
AM													PM
	1	2	2	2									

Group: Preschoolers

GROUP NAME: Preschoolers	AM												PM
NUMBER OF CHILDREN ENROLLED EACH HOUR	6:00	7:00	8:00	9:00	10:00	11:00	12:00	1:00	2:00	3:00	4:00	5:00	6:00	7:00
		4	7/14	18	18	18	18	18	18	18	16/15	15	14/7	

TOTAL NUMBER OF CHILDREN IN GROUP: 18

AGE OF MAJORITY OF CHILDREN IN GROUP: 3½ yr.

HOURS OF EACH STAFF MEMBER:
Janice (7-3)
Karen (11-7)
Gina (8-12)
Claire 2:30-6:30

NUMBER OF TEACHERS PRESENT EACH HOUR													
AM													PM
	1	2	2	2	3	2	2	2/3	2	2	2	2/1	

Group: Older Preschoolers

GROUP NAME: Older Preschoolers	AM												PM
NUMBER OF CHILDREN ENROLLED EACH HOUR	6:00	7:00	8:00	9:00	10:00	11:00	12:00	1:00	2:00	3:00	4:00	5:00	6:00	7:00
		4	8/16	20	20	20	20	20	20	20	20	18	16/8	

TOTAL NUMBER OF CHILDREN IN GROUP: 20

AGE OF MAJORITY OF CHILDREN IN GROUP: 4½ yr.

HOURS OF EACH STAFF MEMBER:
Laura (7-3)
Marsha (11-7)
Hannah (8-12)
Alice (2:30-6:30)

NUMBER OF TEACHERS PRESENT EACH HOUR													
AM													PM
	1	2	2	2	3	2	2	3/2	2	2	2	2/1	

Group: School-agers

GROUP NAME: School-agers	AM												PM
NUMBER OF CHILDREN ENROLLED EACH HOUR	6:00	7:00	8:00	9:00	10:00	11:00	12:00	1:00	2:00	3:00	4:00	5:00	6:00	7:00
		5	8				7	7	7/15	20/26	26	26/20	20/10	

TOTAL NUMBER OF CHILDREN IN GROUP: 26

AGE OF MAJORITY OF CHILDREN IN GROUP: 7 yr

HOURS OF EACH STAFF MEMBER:
Eva (7-9)
Eva (12-2:30)
Judy (1-7)
Mike (2:30-6:30)

NUMBER OF TEACHERS PRESENT EACH HOUR													
AM													PM
	1	1	—	—	—	—	1	2	2	2	2	2/1	

Qualified personnel

The second parameter of the full cost of quality deals with the qualifications and specialized knowledge of educational personnel, including teacher-caregivers, assistants, and the director. When programs include additional personnel such as an assistant director, educational coordinator, or other individuals fulfilling specialty roles, their qualifications also need to be considered.

Personnel must have appropriate qualifications for their roles and responsibilities. Specialized professional preparation is an essential key to program quality; educational staff must understand how children learn and how to teach them appropriately. NAEYC recommends that all individuals working with children have preparation in early childhood education and child development. NAEYC further recommends that individuals in charge of a group of children have a **minimum** of a Child Development Associate Credential (CDA) or an associate degree in early childhood education or child development. Directors should should possess at **minimum** a baccalaureate degree in early childhood education or child development; at least 3 years of teaching experience; and specific preparation in program administration, including financial and human resource management.

In many centers currently, the roles and responsibilities fulfilled by teaching personnel fall into two broad categories: teachers and assistants or aides. This structure offers little opportunity for career development. As a result, teachers with high levels of preparation and experience may earn little more than their novice co-workers. The full cost model is based on a differentiated staffing plan with four categories. A differentiated staffing structure recognizes differences in levels of preparation and practice. Typically the lead teacher of the teaching team has a higher level of preparation and thus commands a higher salary. By creating a career ladder, differentiated staffing patterns encourage other members of the teaching staff to seek further professional preparation.

Teacher-caregivers in family child care who work alone obviously do not employ a differentiated staffing structure; they fulfill all roles and responsibilities themselves. As with center personnel,

---

SUGGESTED EDUCATIONAL ROLES
IN A DIFFERENTIATED STAFFING STRUCTURE

Master teachers have demonstrated excellence in early childhood knowledge and practice. They are responsible for the care and education of a group of children and may supervise and mentor other teaching staff.

Teachers are responsible for the care and education of a group of children. They plan and implement the curriculum, supervise other members of the teaching staff assigned to the group, work with parents, and assess the needs of individual children for incorporation into curriculum planning.

Assistant teachers are responsible for implementing program activities as a part of a teaching team and sharing responsibility for the care and education of a group of children. They assist in the planning and implementation of the curriculum, working with parents, and assessing the needs of individual children.

Teaching assistants assist in the implementation of program activities under the direct supervision of teachers or assistant teachers.

DIFFERENTIATED STAFFING STRUCTURE FOR EDUCATIONAL PERSONNEL WITH SUGGESTED EDUCATIONAL QUALIFICATIONS

Staff Role	Relevant Master's	Relevant Bachelor's	Relevant Associate's	CDA Credential	Some Training	No Training
Director	←	Degree and 3 years experience				
Master Teacher	←	Degree and 3 years experience				
Teacher	←					
Assistant Teacher		←				
Teaching Assistant			←			

This table does not include specialty roles such as educational coordinator, social services coordinator, or other providers of special services. Individuals fulfilling these roles should possess the knowledge and qualifications required to fulfill their responsibilities effectively.

family child care providers are better prepared to work with young children when they have specialized knowledge of early childhood education and child development. The minimum recommended level for a family child care provider is that of an assistant teacher.

The table above portrays the framework of a differentiated staffing structure, listing recommended levels of professional preparation for each role. Consider this information as you complete the **Staff Roles and Educational Qualifications Worksheet (#2).** As illustrated in the sample on the next page, this worksheet is designed to identify the current roles and responsibilities of the program's educational staff.

Additional personnel

The educational staff will include the majority of personnel in many early childhood centers, but additional staff are also needed. Admin-

WORKSHEET #2: STAFF ROLES AND EDUCATIONAL QUALIFICATIONS

Directions: To complete worksheet, list all personnel fulfilling administrative, teaching, support and specialty roles and list relevant educational qualifications. Compare listed qualifications for those recommended for various positions on page 70. If an individual's degree is not in the field, but they have substantial coursework in the field, list qualifications under that degree.

Staff Role	Relevant Master's	Relevant Bachelor's	Relevant Associate's	CDA Credential	Some Training	No Training
Diana, director	✓ and 7 yrs. exp.					
Mary, master teacher		✓+5 yrs exp.				
Angie, teacher				✓ + 5 yrs. exp.		
Julia, teaching asst.					✓	
Ann, teaching asst.					✓	
Sarah, asst. tchr				✓ also working on A.A.		

istrative support is essential. Larger programs often have an assistant director and/or educational coordinator. All-day programs generally require a cook and possibly assistants. Janitorial staff or services are also needed. Other staff will depend on the nature of the services provided. For example, programs offering an array of comprehensive services need staff who have the necessary qualifications for providing family support, health services, or other comprehensive services. Finally, total personnel costs should incorporate the need for substitutes to cover those times when regular staff are not available.

Compensation

Adequate compensation is critical if programs are to recruit and retain qualified employees. As the results of the National Child Care Staffing Study (Whitebook et al., 1990) so clearly indicate, inadequate compensation has a direct and negative impact on the quality of program provided to children.

NAEYC's recently adopted guidelines for compensation of early childhood professionals (see Chapter 5) call for compensation that is comparable within the early childhood profession and across other professions. Currently early childhood professionals employed in the public schools typically receive significantly higher compensation than those employed in private or public programs not funded through the public tax base. Reaching comparability within the early childhood profession is a critical but insufficient step, as kindergarten and primary teachers will be quick to attest. It is also important to consider the compensation received by other professionals within the community who have equivalent educational qualifications and job responsibilities.

NAEYC's compensation guidelines include family child care providers when calling for comparable compensation within the early childhood profession and across other professions. The recommended compensation level depends upon the provider's level of professional preparation and should be comparable to the compensation received by other professionals with similar qualifications and responsibilities. Because family child care providers are for the most part self-employed, their "compensation" is the difference between their income and their business expenses. As with owners of centers who also fulfill a teaching or administrative role, family child care providers should include a comparable level of compensation for themselves when calculating program expenses and determining needed revenue.

The following page lists salaries for different roles within an early childhood program along with those of comparable professionals. These figures reflect national averages. Given the considerable variation that exists from one community or another, programs will be best served by doing local comparisons. Annual teacher salaries for different regions of the country are presented for rough estimates of the degree of regional variation.

Given the considerable variation that exists from one community or another, programs will be best served by doing local comparisons of compensation.

TABLES OF SALARY COMPARABILITY ACROSS PROFESSIONS

PROGRAM DIRECTOR

Early Childhood Program Director (GAO)	$24,340
Public School Principal	
Elementary	$45,900
Secondary	$52,900
Educational Administrators	$35,000
Health Services Managers	$30,524
Personnel Managers	$34,600

TEACHER

Early childhood teacher (GAO)	$14,100
Public School Teacher	$28,900
Registered Nurse	
Experienced; in Hospitals	$32,100
Entry; in Hospitals	$23,100
Median; in Nursing Homes	$21,300
Social Worker	
Median	$22,000
With M.S.W.	$27,700
Personnel, Training, and Labor Relations Specialists	$26,400

TEACHER ASSISTANTS/AIDES

Early Childhood Assistant (GAO)	$10,200
Licensed Practical Nurse	
In Hospitals	$17,500
In Nursing Homes	$15,000
Teacher Aide	$14,664
Nursing Aide	$11,500

Unless otherwise noted, all salaries are annual median salaries for the profession. The source of these data is the 1990 Occupational Outlook Handbook, U.S. Department of Labor. Salaries are reported salaries; for many school personnel, salary is based on a school year not a full year; annualized data would be higher.

The **Worksheet on Comparable Salaries (#3)** provides a tool for identifying a range of comparable compensation packages within the community to allow an individual program or community to determine estimates for "improved" and "full cost" salaries for individuals at different levels of job responsibility.

Having determined salary figures for different job responsibilities, it is now possible to compute individual salaries. NAEYC's compensation guidelines recommend that individual salaries provide for merit increases and continued professional development. Recognizing mastery in practice and knowledge through differential salaries establishes a career ladder, and encourages individuals to pursue professional growth. The figures computed in the worksheet on comparability represent **average** salaries for a position. Individual salaries may be computed following consideration of the individual's specific qualifications and performance. Use the **Worksheet for Determining Total Compensation Costs (#4)** to estimate individual salaries of all personnel.

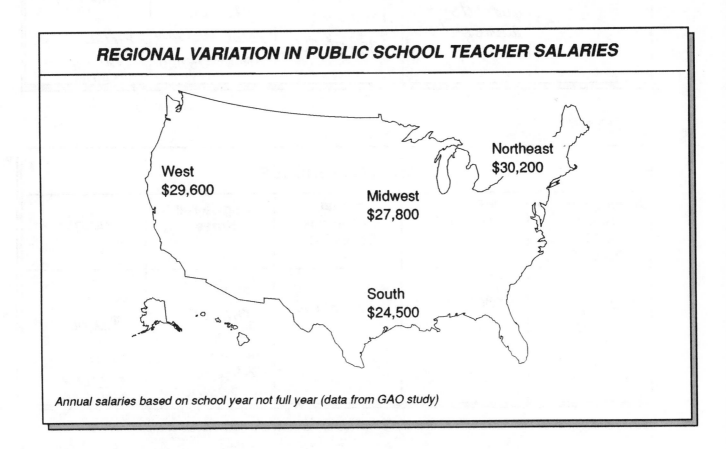

REGIONAL VARIATION IN PUBLIC SCHOOL TEACHER SALARIES

Northeast
$30,200

West
$29,600

Midwest
$27,800

South
$24,500

Annual salaries based on school year not full year (data from GAO study)

WORKSHEET #3: COMPARING SALARIES FOR VARIOUS POSITIONS WITH COMPARABLE PROFESSIONALS WITHIN THE COMMUNITY

This worksheet should be used to compare staff positions requiring different levels of educational preparation and responsibility to comparable professionals within the community. Family child care providers should choose the position most comparable to their current levels of educational preparation and responsibility. This information may then be used to estimate a target salary level. Some programs may choose to identify a series of steps to reach the full cost target.

DIRECTOR				
Current Average Salary DIRECTOR	Public School Principal	Human Resources Manager	Health Services Administrator	TARGET
$24,300	3 local school districts — average is $45,000	5 local industries — range is $32-38,000	Community hospital — $45,000 local nursing home- $25,000	INITIAL — $35,000 FINAL — $40,000 plus inflation

MASTER TEACHER				
Current Average Salary MASTER TEACHER	Public School Teacher*	Human Resources Specialist*	Registered Nurse*	TARGET
$16,000	$30-35,000	$28-31,000	hospital — $31,000 nursing home — $22,000	INITIAL — $22,000 FINAL — $33,000 + inflation

*Base comparisons on individuals with comparable advanced preparation and higher levels of experience.

TEACHER				
Current Average Salary for TEACHER	Public School Teacher*	Human Resources Specialist*	Registered Nurse*	TARGET
$14,100	district average is $28,000	$22-27,500	hospital — $27,500 nursing home — $21,000	INITIAL — $20,000 FINAL — $30,000 plus inflation

Base comparisons on individuals with comparable preparation and levels of experience.

ASSISTANT TEACHER				
Current Average Salary for ASST. TEACHER	Public School Asst. Teacher	Human Resources Assistant	Registered Nurse or Licensed Practical Nurse	TARGET
$12,000	$20-22,000	$17,500 – 21,000	hospital — $17,500 $15,000 in nursing home	INITIAL — $16,000 FINAL — $23,000 + inflation

Base comparisons on individuals with comparable preparation and levels of experience.

TEACHING ASSISTANT				
Current Average Salary for TEACHING ASST.	Public School Teacher Aide*	Human Resources Office Assistant*	Nurse's Aide*	TARGET
$10,000	$17,500	$13,000 – 15,500	$11,500	INITIAL — $13,500 FINAL — $17,500 + inflation

Base comparisons on individuals with comparable preparation and levels of experience.

WORKSHEET #4: DETERMINING TOTAL COMPENSATION COSTS

Directions: To complete worksheet, list all personnel fulfilling administrative, teaching, support and specialty roles. General target salary is based on average comparable salary for the individual's role from Worksheet #3. Individual Target Salaries should be determined taking into account the individual's level of qualification and mastery of performance.

To estimate benefits: MULITIPLY Total Salaries by .20 or .25 to determine total benefits. depending on desired level (20% or 25%).

Staff member	Current Salary	General Target (from Wksht. #3)	Individual Target
Mary	$16,000	$22,000	$23,000
Angie	$14,100	$16,000	$16,500
Julia	$10,000	$13,500	$13,500
Total Salaries			
Benefits			
TOTAL COMPENSATION			

Completed for Initial Targets

Benefits

The provision of an adequate benefits package is an essential part of an overall compensation package. Benefits not only provide considerable value to an individual's compensation, but their provision can greatly enhance working conditions and job satisfaction. In the earlier national estimates, the cost of benefits (including taxes) for accredited programs was estimated at 13% of total compensation costs, based on GAO findings. For the "improved" cost calculations, benefits were based on 16.3% of total compensation. This figure is the national average value of benefits packages as a proportion of total compensation, excluding paid leave (Employee Benefit Research Institute, 1990). This works out to be approximately 20% of salary. At full cost, benefits are estimated at a slightly more liberal 25% of salary. These calculations are based on salaries for a 52-week year. As a result, leave time is calculated as part of salary rather than benefits. If leave is not calculated into salary, benefits should represent a higher percentage of the total compensation package.

Free or reduced cost child care is a benefit increasingly offered by employers. It may be particularly attractive to early childhood staff, since most are women of childbearing age. However, if the space provided as a benefit could be filled by another child with paid tuition, the child care benefit represents lost income to the program. The NCCSS (Whitebook et al. 1990) found that programs providing free child care to their employees tended to be of lower quality than programs not providing that benefit.

The calculation of salaries and benefits provides the basic determinants of personnel costs. The **Worksheet of Total Compensation Costs (#4)** may be completed by adding in the costs of benefits. The sum of this worksheet represents total personnel costs.

Because family child care providers are self-employed, desired benefits must be calculated into the costs of program provision, for example, the costs of contributions to an individual retirement account and the costs of a substitute to provide vacation and sick leave. Family child care providers may receive some benefits by being self-employed in their own home. For example, home owners may be able to depreciate space and equipment as business expenses. (This also applies to owners of centers.) For family child care providers with young children, there may be significant benefits to being at home with their own children. At first glance, it may appear that these providers save child care expenses. However, providers' children represent foregone income if additional children could be served.

RECOMMENDED BENEFITS

Paid leave (annual, holidays, sick, and/or personal)

Medical insurance

Retirement

Educational stipends

The provision of an adequate benefits package is an essential part of an overall compensation package.

ASSESSING THE LEARNING ENVIRONMENT FOR CHILDREN

1. Are the indoor and outdoor environments safe, clean, attractive, and spacious? Is there a **minimum** of 35 square feet of usable playroom floor space indoors and a **minimum** of 75 square feet of play space outdoors per child?

2. Do staff have access to the space in sufficient time to prepare the environment for children?

3. Do all groups have access to a wide variety of age-appropriate materials and equipment?

4. Are there individual spaces for children to hang their clothing and store their personal belongings?

5. Are there soft elements in the environment—bacterial-resistant rugs, cushions, or rocking chairs?

6. Are sound-absorbing materials used to reduce excessive noise?

   Noise is to be expected in a high quality program for children. Acoustical building materials, carpet, and other sound-absorbing materials can create a more pleasant environment for learning and working by reducing excessive noise.

7. Does the outdoor area include a variety of surfaces—soil, sand, grass, hills, flat sections, and hard areas for wheel toys?

8. Does the outdoor area include shade; open space; digging space; and a variety of equipment for riding, climbing, balancing, and individual play?

   While all of these elements may not occur naturally in the outdoor environment, equipment and other materials may be used to provide a variety of surfaces and shaded areas.

9. Is the outdoor area fenced or protected by natural barriers from streets and other dangerous areas?

10. Are the equipment and materials for indoor as well as outdoor play safe and well-maintained?

11. Are all indoor and outdoor facilities kept in a safe, clean condition and in good repair?

   Checklist adapted from NAEYC accreditation Criteria

ESTABLISHING A GOOD ENVIRONMENT

A good learning environment for children

Attention to environmental aspects can make a big difference in the degree to which children's learning is enhanced, both directly through the provision of space and resources and indirectly through the positive impact of good working conditions on adults' interactions with children. A good learning environment for children is spacious and offers ample room—indoors and out—for learning. The materials and equipment are sufficient in number; are appropriate to the ages and needs of children; and are safe, clean, and in good repair. The checklist above may be used to assess the quality of the children's learning environment.

A good working environment for adults

In addition to specific features of the children's learning environment, it is critical to examine the nature of the adult working environment. A good working environment not only helps to recruit and retain qualified staff, but can greatly affect the quality of staff-child relationships. Overstressed and unhappy teacher-caregivers find it difficult, if not impossible, to provide the warm, nurturing care and attention so essential to children's learning and well-being.

The checklist on staff working conditions addresses aspects of the physical work environment as the psychological environment. These questions are best answered independently by staff members. An administrator's or outsider's perception of working conditions may be significantly different than that of a specific employee. It is also crucial that all staff have the opportunity to respond to these questions, not just a select group of personnel.

ASSESSING THE ADULT WORKING ENVIRONMENT

1. Is space provided for staff to store personal belongings?

2. Is there a staff lounge or private area providing a comfortable place to relax away from children?

3. Is there a staff development library and resource center?

4. Does the program provide sufficient resources so that teachers do not need to purchase supplies and equipment for learning activities out of their personal budget?

5. Are staff who work directly with children provided breaks of at least 15 minutes in each 4-hour period?

6. Are there written personnel policies, including job descriptions, compensation, resignation and termination, benefits, and grievance procedures? Are policies clearly communicated to staff members?

7. Is accident protection and liability insurance coverage maintained for adults as well as children?

8. Is there frequent communication among staff and administrators?

9. Are there regular staff meetings for staff to consult on program planning, plan for individual children, and discuss working conditions?

10. Are new staff adequately oriented about the goals and philosophy of the program, emergency procedures, special needs of children, guidance and classroom management techniques, and planned daily activities in the program?

Checklist adapted from NAEYC accreditation Criteria.

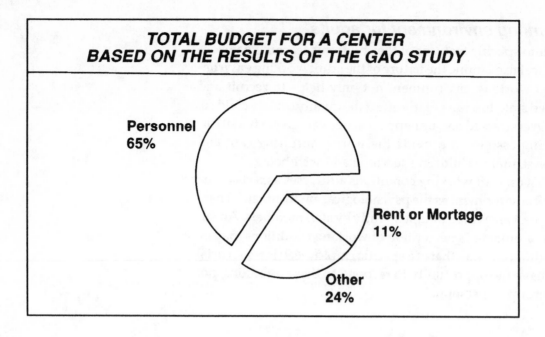

**TOTAL BUDGET FOR A CENTER
BASED ON THE RESULTS OF THE GAO STUDY**

Personnel
65%

Rent or Mortage
11%

Other
24%

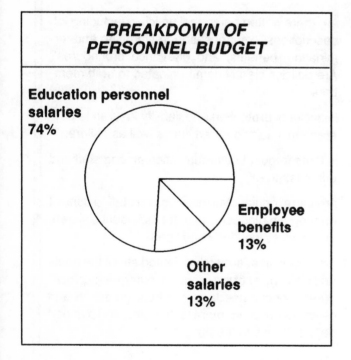

**BREAKDOWN OF
PERSONNEL BUDGET**

Education personnel
salaries
74%

Employee
benefits
13%

Other
salaries
13%

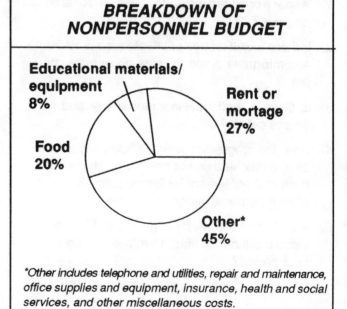

**BREAKDOWN OF
NONPERSONNEL BUDGET**

Educational materials/
equipment
8%

Rent or
mortage
27%

Food
20%

Other*
45%

*Other includes telephone and utilities, repair and maintenance,
office supplies and equipment, insurance, health and social
services, and other miscellaneous costs.*

ESTIMATING THE TOTAL PROGRAM BUDGET

Completing the various worksheets throughout this chapter provides a great deal of information for estimating both the current and full cost budget, but more information is needed. The chart on the opposite page illustrates the major budget categories identified by the GAO study of accredited centers in relation to the full cost parameters. Depending upon the type and amount of contributed goods and services, an individual program budget may differ markedly from this breakdown.

Worksheet #5 presents a general format for listing typical program expenses. The categories are adapted from a cost-modeling study of early childhood programs by Richard Clifford and Susan Russell (1989). The categories may need further adaptation for a particular program. In addition to personnel, typical categories include occupancy, administration, and educational program costs. Insurance costs are included under administration. Educational program costs include expenses to ensure a developmentally appropriate program for children. Included are costs for educational supplies and equipment, staff development, parent involvement, and field trips. Other expenses related to program include nutrition and food service, supplementary social services, and transportation. In order to fully capture the total costs of program provision, it is important to consider the value of contributions and in-kind donations. To adequately capture these values, the second column on the worksheet asks for an estimate of the market value of the good or service. For example, a program may pay a fee for space, but at substantially below market rate. The difference between the actual cost and market cost is the value of the subsidy that the program is receiving. A separate budget sheet has been prepared by Kathy Modigliani for use by family child care providers.

The costs of program provision may be divided by the total number of children served to gain an estimate of the cost per child. However, such an estimate may be misleading, given the considerable differential in costs for providing services for children of different ages. The fact that services for infants and toddlers are extremely labor-intensive, for example, makes their costs significantly higher. Thus, most programs and decision makers find it most useful to consider costs per child separately for different age groups. A rough estimate may be obtained by separating personnel costs for teachers by dividing the teaching personnel costs based on the age of children served and splitting all remaining costs equally among the age groups.

It is important to consider the value of contributions and in-kind donations.

Additional costs for for-profit programs

As Culkin, Helburn, and Morris describe in Chapter 2, differences in program type can result in large cost differences, in part due to differential access to various forms of subsidy. For example, for-profit programs must pay taxes. For-profit programs may be subject to com-

WORKSHEET #5: BUDGET OF EARLY CHILDHOOD PROGRAM COSTS

BUDGET CATEGORY	CURRENT EXPENSES	ESTIMATED MARKET COSTS	SUBSIDY (Market less current costs)
PERSONNEL COSTS Director			
Other Educational/Support Specialists			
Teaching Staff			
Administrative Support Staff			
Other staff (cook, janitor, etc.)			
Substitutes/temporary labor			
TOTAL SALARIES			
BENEFITS			
PERSONNEL TAXES (FICA/Unemployment)			
TOTAL PERSONNEL COSTS			
OCCUPANCY COSTS Rent/Mortage			
Utilities			
Janitorial Service/Supplies			
Building/Grounds Maintenance			
TOTAL OCCUPANCY COSTS			
ADMINISTRATIVE COSTS Insurance (liability/property/theft/accident/etc.)			
Office Equipment (Copier/typewriter/computer and software/telephone and answering machine/etc.)			
Advertising			
Postage			
Licensing/Organizational Fees			
Taxes			
TOTAL ADMINISTRATIVE COSTS			

Budget, continued

BUDGET OF EARLY CHILDHOOD PROGRAM COSTS, CONTINUED			
BUDGET CATEGORY	**CURRENT EXPENSES**	**ESTIMATED MARKET COSTS**	**SUBSIDY** (Market less current costs)
EDUCATIONAL PROGRAM COSTS			
Program supplies			
Program equipment			
Staff development			
Parent involvement			
Field trips			
Nutrition and food service			
Transportation			
Supplementary social services			
(Health/dental screening; vision/hearing screening; speech/language therapy; support services for serving children with special needs)			
Equipment/resources to support services for children with special needs			
TOTAL EDUCATIONAL PROGRAM COSTS			
TOTAL COSTS OF SERVICE PROVISION (add shaded areas)			

EQUITABLE FAMILY CHILD CARE BUDGET (ANNUAL EXPENSES)
Developed by Kathy Modigliani, Bank Street College

	TOTAL (Add shaded areas)
PERSONNEL *Equitable wages (estimate of wages that a person with similar education, experience, and reponsibilities would earn in other jobs in the community)* Provider Assistants and substitutes Other (e.g., Custodian*)	
TOTAL WAGES	
Benefits @ 25% of Wages	
TOTAL COMPENSATION (Wages & Benefits)	
FOOD	
Supplies and Equipment Toys and materials Office supplies, computer Household supplies* Equipment*	
TOTAL SUPPLIES AND EQUIPMENT	
Other Expenses Postage Copying Maintenance and repairs* Rent/Mortage, Utilities* Insurance Advertising Accountant Business entertaining/gifts Mileage/transportation Professional dues and publications Professional conference expenses	
TOTAL OTHER EXPENSES	
GRAND TOTAL	

Prorate the family child care portion of these expenses

To determine the Full Cost per child for full-time care, divide total expenses by the full-time equivalent number of children in the program. This is the full cost of full-time care that is not subsidized by the provider. ***Kathy Modigliani*** *is a member of the NAEYC Advisory Panel on Quality, Compensation, and Affordability.*

mercial zoning requirements, resulting in higher costs than if the program were located in a residential area. Higher apparent costs may be incurred by for-profit programs because they are less likely to receive donations, material or in-kind, since there is no tax incentive for making the donation.

ESTIMATING THE FULL COST OF QUALITY

To estimate the costs for full quality, **Worksheet #6** combines questions posed throughout this chapter in relation to each of the parameters of full cost. This worksheet may be used to identify needs, list options, and decide on the most feasible course of action. Assuming these changes are made, **Worksheet #7** repeats the budget categories in Worksheet #5 to estimate the Full Cost budget.

WHERE DOES THE MONEY COME FROM?

The full cost figures may prove shocking to many program decision makers. They certainly are considerably higher than the often-cited $3,000 annual cost of care. The difference between current cost and full cost for most programs will reflect the increased personnel costs of comparable compensation based on educational qualifications and job responsibilities. As described in Chapter 2, the foregone wages of staff represent the most common existing subsidy utilized by early childhood programs. Essentially, the full cost of quality campaign seeks to transfer the subsidy provided by early childhood teachers to other sources. The question, however, is to whom can these costs be transferred.

Families are not the answer

Although it is imperative that the subsidy of early childhood programs be shifted from early childhood personnel, it is clear that most families cannot be expected to pay the full cost of quality. Undoubtedly, some families can afford to pay more than they are currently paying. But, the lack of affordable, quality early care and education programs is a major issue facing too many American families. New federal child care assistance, especially through the federal child care block grant and through welfare and job training programs, should help to make child care more affordable. For the most part, however, new aid is targeted to families with incomes below the state median income; additional support continues to be needed by many families at or above 75% of the state median income.

A growing number of employers have become involved in the provision of early childhood services. Ideally, the new federal program will continue to stimulate such investments. In both public and private investments, the primary has been on "demand side" subsidies as opposed to "supply side" subsidies. When subsidies are calculated on the current price for the purchase of care, they severely underestimate the costs of service provision. The NCCSS and GAO

Reaching the full cost of quality in early childhood programs will depend on greater use of supply subsidies to better cover the true costs of program provision.

WORKSHEET #6: CHANGES NEEDED TO REACH FULL QUALITY

PROGRAM CHARACTERISTICS: NEEDED IMPROVEMENTS	OPTIONS FOR CHANGE	COST
PROMOTING GOOD RELATIONSHIPS *Limited group size; good adult-child ratios; continuity in staffing* Infants & toddlers grouped together at end of day and group is too big.	hire part-time worker to come in afternoons — check if college work-study student in ECE available.	
QUALIFIED STAFF WITH SPECIALIZED PREPARATION IN CHILD DEVELOPMENT/ EARLY EDUCATION *Staff appropriately prepared for level of responsibility; ongoing program for staff development* Staff can't afford to attend professional conferences. Toddler teachers need specialized training for age group. All staff could use more training.	Plan fund-raising event to cover travel & registration. Arrange in-service session on toddlers Reimburse staff for tuition of one course per semester.	

PROGRAM CHARACTERISTICS: STRENGTHS AND WEAKNESSES	OPTIONS FOR CHANGE	COST
ADEQUATE COMPENSATION *Staff compensation comparable to similar community professionals; good benefits package provided; career ladder in place* Little reward in salary for tenure or performance. Salaries about half of local school district for comparable preparation & responsibility.	Institute a career ladder; tie salary increases to level of preparation and performance. Target fee increase to salary improvement.	
ESTABLISHING A GOOD ENVIRONMENT **FOR CHILDREN TO LEARN** *Safe, well-maintained facility with ample space and equipment; sufficient variety of developmentally appropriate learning materials and equipment provided through program budget* Teachers provide supplies largely out of their own budget. Windows drafty — need replacing. **FOR ADULTS TO WORK** *Staff lounge; personal storage areas; paid breaks; good working conditions; staff development and resource library available* No staff lounge	Increase supply budget. Replace 2 worst windows this years — others next year. Clean out front storage area. Ask parents to help renovate by painting. Get second-hand sofa & chairs. Provide coffee and install telephone.	

studies found that parent fees represent only about 70 to 75% of actual costs. These costs include only what Culkin, Helburn, and Morris describe as apparent costs; they do not take into account in-kind donations, much less the hidden subsidy of early childhood teachers through foregone wages.

Reaching the full cost of quality in early childhood programs will depend on greater use of supply subsidies to better cover the true costs of program provision. Such approaches will be most successful when approached from a community-wide or state coalition. A number of such approaches are outlined in the following chapter as suggested activities for coalitions joining forces to reach the full cost of quality.

Reaching the full cost of quality cannot be accomplished overnight; it will take time, persistence, and dedication. But, it is an effort that must be pursued by all early childhood programs and all advocates concerned with the well-being of young children and their families. Assuming that the full cost of quality is too expensive to achieve passes the burden on to our children, because they ultimately pay the price of lower program quality that results from the ever growing difficulties in recruiting and retaining qualified staff. Planning strategies for moving toward—and ultimately achieving—the full cost of quality is a necessity if we as a nation are to effectively prepare this generation of young children to succeed in school and to become effectively functioning adults in our society. Paying the full costs of quality will be a significant investment, but the future costs of not providing for our children today will be even higher. And, like all good investments, an investment in quality for young children will reap dividends many times the original cost.

REFERENCES

Bredekamp, S. (Ed.). (1987). *Accreditation criteria and procedures of the National Academy of Early Childhood Programs.* Washington, DC: NAEYC.

Clifford, R.M., & Russell, S. D. (1989) Financing programs for preschool-aged children. *Theory into Practice,* 28(1).

Employee Benefit Research Institute (1990). EBRI databook on employee benefits. Washington, DC: Author.

U.S. Department of Laobr, Bureau of Labor Statistics (1990). *Occupational outlook handbook,* 1990–91 edition. Washington, DC: U.S. Government Printing Office.

U.S. General Accounting Office. (1990). *Briefing Report to the Chairman, Committee on Labor and Human Resources, U.S. Senate. Early Childhood Education. What are the costs of high-quality programs?* Washington, DC: Author.

Whitebook, M., Howes, C., & Phillips, D. (1990). *Who cares? Child care teachers and the quality of care in America.* Oakland, CA: Child Care Employee Project.

Reaching the full cost of quality cannot be accomplished overnight; it will take time, persistence, and dedication.

Developing a Coalition to Reach the Full Cost of Quality

7

Joan Lombardi

DIVERSITY. No word better describes both the variety of early childhood programs today and the groups of people now showing interest in child care and other early childhood services. Yet, a common thread has emerged among the patchwork of program types and the growing number of interested groups: concern for quality.

The need to improve quality across all types of early childhood programs, using multiple sources of funding, requires collective action. Coalitions provide the vehicle for such collaboration. When a variety of groups successfully collaborate, they work together. They try to find common goals. They pool their individual energies and resources to strengthen their voice and their effectiveness. They remain flexible to new ideas. They reach across the artificial boundaries that divide them and focus on their shared goal to improve services for children and families.

This chapter briefly defines a coalition, presents a series of questions to help coalition members think through the issues before them, and provides examples of strategies for action. This material is specifically designed for a coalition or subcommittee which is focused on reaching the full cost of quality in early childhood programs. Suggested strategies include improving professional and regulatory standards, expanding training opportunities, and increasing funding for staff compensation and improved parental access to and recognition of quality care. Rather than providing a specific prescription for organizing a coalition and its activities, this discussion is designed to facilitate the "process" of coalition building and action planning in a way that respects community needs, while helping to reach the full cost of quality.

Coalitions are alliances established to achieve a particular goal.

CONVENING A COALITION

Coalitions are alliances among groups and/or individuals which are established to achieve a particular goal. Some coalitions are temporary, lasting only until a specific goal is accomplished, for example, passage of a piece of legislation or to develop a plan of action on a particular subject. Other coalitions may develop into permanent organizations with ongoing responsibility and staff. In either case, such groups may be called by a variety of names including coalition, alliance, council, or committee.

Coalitions grow in many ways, both at the state and community level. They may emerge as a result of networking among early childhood program directors or parents, or through the efforts of the local or state child care resource and referral or early childhood professional organizations. In other cases, the coalition may result from a recommendation made by a public official, business leader, or civic group. Although we often think of coalitions as functioning outside of government, many new early childhood legislative proposals establish interagency coordinating bodies which often address similar issues.

Membership in the coalition

The way in which a coalition emerges may determine the group's composition and purpose, the responsibility for group leadership, and its available resources. Some child care coalitions only include organizations that are directly related to service provision for young children. Since strategies to improve quality will need broad community support, the most effective coalitions reach out to a wider variety of groups.

The size of a coalition will also vary. Some coalitions have 10 to 15 members, while others may have 100 or more. Large coalitions need steering committees or other mechanisms for planning and leadership. Consensus building, access to resources, and planned activities are enhanced by all members' input. Other tasks are generally accomplished more efficiently when delegated to smaller committees or task forces. The number of coalition

---

QUESTIONS TO ASK WHEN RECRUITING COALITION MEMBERS

- What organizations are involved in providing early childhood services?

- What groups are affected by early childhood programs or have a vested interest in the early childhood delivery system?

- What groups or individuals hold prominent roles in the community and have an influence over public or private policies?

- What organizations can contribute to the diversity of the coalition?

POTENTIAL COALITION MEMBERS

- Parents or groups representing parents

- Teachers and administrators of programs for young children in all types of centers—nonprofit, for-profit, church-related, etc., family child care, Head Start, and in public schools

- Resource and referral agencies

- Related service providers (pediatricians, other health services)

- Organizations of providers (AEYC Affiliate Groups or other early childhood organizations, Head Start Associations, and family child care associations and networks)

- Early childhood trainers and researchers in colleges, universities, or other agencies

- Civic groups

- Religious groups

- Corporations in the community and organizations representing the interests of local or state businesses and labor

- Voluntary service organizations

- Philanthropic organizations, including community foundations

- Public officials

---

members may change from time to time. Coalitions are often fluid; membership sometimes changes as priorities shift or in response to specific issues.

Ingredients of a successful coalition

Joining a coalition means making a commitment to work with others on a common goal. Working through issues with others in a group calls for an ability to listen and share, to maintain your own identity while pursuing common objectives, to be willing to take a stand, yet be flexible enough to compromise. In very diverse

---

INITIAL QUESTIONS FOR COALITION MEMBERS

- How will working in a coalition be different from working within an individual organization?

- How can coalition members best be supportive of each other and respect individual differences?

- How will decisions be made?

- What steps can be taken to ensure the active participation of all coalition members?

- What mechanisms will be used for self-evaluation and feedback among members?

---

groups, this process is often time consuming and difficult, yet can bring long term benefits and important changes in the early childhood system.

The more diverse the makeup of the coalition and the perspectives it represents, the stronger its voice. Therefore, coalition members must be willing to accept differences in opinions, values, attitudes, and communication styles. They must be willing to share power and see other organizations, large or small, as their peers.

Discussing the questions above will help all members share a common understanding of their roles and functions with the coalition. These issues should be discussed not only in a coalition's beginning stages, but need ongoing clarification throughout the life of the coalition.

Effective leadership

The leadership role in a coalition is critical to its success. Many coalitions have a chairperson who is either elected by the group or appointed by the organization or person convening the coalition. An effective leader helps the group to remain focused on its goal, guides the group, stimulates discussion, and helps the group move forward on issues. Good leaders recognize and appreciate the various personalities in a group and attempt to facilitate their active participation. An effective chairperson makes sure that all perspectives are aired before a decision is reached. During the discussion, effective leaders maintain a low profile and do not attempt to impose their particular views on others. Finally, a strong leader promotes leadership among members.

The more diverse the makeup of the coalition and the perspectives it represents, the stronger its voice.

GETTING STARTED: ESTABLISHING GOALS, ASSESSING NEEDS, AND DEVELOPING A VISION

The initial stage of a coalition's work is often considered a planning period. During this stage the group spends time thinking about the purpose of their work and establishing general goals. Next, they take stock of the current status of the quality of early childhood services in the community or state by assessing needs. Finally, before setting out to make changes, they develop a vision of what they want and establish specific goals.

Establishing overall goals

Once a coalition is convened, members need time to get to know each other, to find common ground, and to come to consensus on the coalition's goals. During initial meetings, it will be useful for coalition members to discuss questions designed to ensure that they share a common purpose.

QUESTIONS FOR ESTABLISHING GOALS

- Why is your organization concerned about quality?

- What do you see as important elements of quality?

- What changes do you think are needed in the community?

- How much effort (time and resources) is your organization willing to contribute?

- Is your organization willing to support a range of strategies that benefit a variety of service providers?

Develop a vision of what you want before taking action.

Assessing needs

Although overall goals will be developed early on, a specific plan of action will most likely emerge through a more intensive evaluation of community needs and resources. Such a needs assessment can provide an overall picture of where the community stands on the elements of quality, including regulatory and professional standards, training, compensation, and parental access to and recognition of quality services. A subcommittee of the coalition may take responsibility for assessing overall needs or various subcommittees may focus on different elements of quality. It will be important for coalition members to have specific tasks in order to encourage their active participation and give momentum to the coalition. The following lists possible questions for coalitions to use in discussions, surveys, focus groups, or hearings to assess needs and to establish priorities.

QUESTIONS FOR ASSESSING COMMUNITY NEEDS

Regulatory and professional standards

- What are the community and/or state licensing standards affecting centers with regard to staff preservice qualifications? Inservice training? Group size? Ratios?

- What are the community and/or state regulations affecting family child care providers with regard to preservice qualifications? Inservice training? Total number of children allowed? Maximum number of infants? Toddlers?

- Are any providers exempt from public regulation of quality variables?

- What other standards are in place to promote staff qualifications and a career ladder?

- How do these compare to other communities or states? To NAEYC criteria?

- What resources are needed to support licensing and enforcement?

- What percentage of centers in the community are accredited by NAEYC? How many family child care providers are accredited by the National Association of Family Day Care (NAFDC)?

- What percentage of staff, including family child care providers, have a relevant credential or certificate (either the nationally recognized CDA or a state early childhood certificate)?

- In what ways is accreditation, certification, and/or credentialing being encouraged?

Training

- What training opportunities are available for the various roles fulfilled by early childhood personnel (directors, teachers and assistants in center-based programs, family child care providers, and support personnel)?

- What training opportunities are available for providers serving different age groups (infants, toddlers, preschoolers, school-age children) and children with special needs?

- Is training available for providers at various levels (preprofessional and professional)?

- Are training opportunities more readily available for some roles and/or program types? What is the area of greatest need?

- Is training accessible (offered at various times in places throughout the community or on-site)?

- Who provides training (individuals, centers, resource and referral, vocational/technical schools, community colleges, 4-year colleges, graduate schools)? What new types of training institutions are needed?

- Is there a training network or is training coordinated in any way? Is there appropriate articulation among types of training available?

- What is the quality of the training (i.e., Does it include the areas outlined in the Child Development Associate competencies and NAEYC's Criteria for High Quality Early Childhood Programs? Does it integrate classroom and field experiences? Does it provide for a mentor to work with the candidate over a period of time? Does it include competency-based assessment)?

- Are there special issues in this community that should be included in the content of the training?

- Do training opportunities encourage providers to move up a career ladder, leading to a state or nationally recognized credential or certification?

- What resources are available to support trainers and training institutions?

- Are there funds available to support individuals seeking training? What are the sources and limitations?

Compensation

- What are the salaries and benefits of various providers of early childhood services in the community? Are there differences among program types?

- How is compensation affecting turnover and morale of staff and the supply of quality programs?

QUESTIONS FOR ASSESSING COMMUNITY NEEDS, CONTINUED

Compensation, continued

- How does compensation for early childhood staff in community-based programs compare to public school teachers or other professionals in the community?

- Is compensation provided in accordance with NAEYC's Guidelines for the Compensation of Early Childhood Professionals?

- In what ways are early childhood teachers encouraged to advocate for increased compensation?

Parental access to and recognition of quality

- How much do families pay for the various types of child care in this community?

- What support (public and private) is available?

- Are there waiting lists for subsidized child care? Head Start?

- Is there a resource and referral program in the community or a network in the state?

- What resources are available to help families identify and monitor program quality?

- What efforts are being made to provide greater recognition to those that provide quality early childhood services?

Developing a vision

The process of assessing needs will help clarify where the community now stands on critical areas affecting quality. Once the needs assessment is completed, the coalition can move on to establish a specific action agenda to develop policies that promote quality in early childhood programs. Since the coalition process is often more spiral than linear, in reality, coalitions may develop their action agenda as they simultaneously assess needs.

The NAEYC compensation guidelines, accreditation standards, and other position statements can provide important benchmarks to help develop a vision of quality. The checklist on the opposite page includes questions to consider in the four critical areas.

REACHING FOR QUALITY: STRATEGIES FOR ACTION

The process of assessing needs, developing a vision of quality, and reaching consensus, are all steps that lead to concrete action to make change. The following section summarizes the guiding principles or approach to making changes, provides an overview of specific initiatives to reach the full cost of quality, and presents questions for assessing progress.

Guiding principles for action

Strategies to improve quality will vary depending on identified needs and the coalition's available resources. However, there are at least three critical principles applicable to any coalition working to improve early childhood program quality:

CRITICAL ELEMENTS FOR DEVELOPING POLICIES WHICH SUPPORT QUALITY IN EARLY CHILDHOOD PROGRAMS

Standards

- What *qualifications* for preservice and inservice training do you support in public licensing and regulatory systems and in state certification processes?

- What changes do you want to make in standards that affect *staffing* of early childhood programs, including total group size, adult-child ratio, maximum number of infants, and inclusion of the provider's own children in the total number of children allowed in the group.

- What changes do want to make in standards that affect the *environment* for children and staff? Indoor and outdoor space requirements? Requirements promoting improved working conditions?

Training system

- What mechanisms can be established to make more training *available* to early childhood teaching personnel in centers and family child care programs?

- How can training be financed and delivered to make it more *accessible* to those who currently or potentially work in early childhood programs, including family child care?

- How can the training be *coordinated* to promote articulation between the levels of training and networking among training institutions and individual trainers?

- What standards should be incorporated into the training to ensure that both the contents and methods are *effective* for improving early childhood practice?

Compensation

- Is there consensus on *wage scales and benefits* for early childhood personnel, providing increased compensation for higher levels of qualifications and responsibility?

- How can these wage scales or guidelines be *financed* (i.e., higher reimbursement rates, salary enhancement grants, pay equity, etc.)?

Parental access to and recognition of quality

- What strategies and materials should be made available to increase *parents' recognition and understanding of quality* in early childhood programs?

- How can resources be made available to help make quality programs *affordable* to families?

- What strategies are needed to promote the availability of *resource and referral* services to families and the community?

---

1. **The various segments of the early childhood system are interrelated.**

   Changes in one type of early childhood program most often affect the resources and ability of other programs to ensure quality. Strategies should be developed which support improvements across the various types of early childhood programs (centers, family child care, Head Start, and public school programs).

2. **The various elements of quality are interrelated.**

   We must use a holistic approach to improving quality that considers all the elements. Strategies to improve one area (for example, establishing a career ladder) must be accompanied by strategies to affect other areas (for example, providing training resources and adequate compensation as incentives to move up the career ladder). One quality variable should not be sacrificed for another. For example, we should not improve compensation by increasing group size.

3. All sectors of society should support quality.

Reaching the full cost of quality for all segments of the early childhood community will take multiple funding sources. Strategies should include efforts to increase public funding as well as to encourage private investments.

Sample Initiatives to reach the full cost of quality

There is much work to be done to reach the full cost of quality. Because there are so many possible activities in a number of different areas, a coalition should prioritize its efforts. Again, priorities will depend on the nature of the community or state and the resources available. The following pages outline various activities a coalition may consider. Readers are urged to also see *Who Knows How Safe? The Status of State Efforts to Ensure Quality Child Care*, written by Gina Adams and published by the Children's Defense Fund. (See the list of resources, p. 97 for information on this and other sources for further details on implementation.)

POTENTIAL COALITION ACTIVITIES

Establishing a quality improvement fund

- Enlist the public and private sector in developing an overall fund to improve quality.

- Establish criteria for the use of the fund (provide training, pay for accreditation or certification, increase salaries, purchase equipment, etc).

- Establish eligibility requirements for providers interested in the fund.

- Advocate for incentives to promote quality improvements (higher reimbursement rates for accredited programs and certified providers).

Building a training system

- Advocate for improved standards in public regulations, including requirements for pre-service and inservice training, and in state certification processes.

- Support public and professional initiatives to establish a career ladder.

- Launch initiatives to finance the provision of and access to training. Provide funds either directly to *providers* (scholarships or loan forgiveness) or to *trainers* (grants to colleges, resource and referrals, or other institutions offering training). Use creative means to finance (licensing fees, lottery funds, public/private partnerships).

- Develop innovative strategies to increase available training opportunities (mobile libraries; resource centers; site visitors; and use of videos, teleconferencing, cable TV).

- Improve the quality of training (establish training networks, provide new resources for trainers, encourage mentored training that is ongoing, field-based, and addresses the CDA competencies).

- Promote articulation across training institutions so that individuals may accumulate credits toward the acquisition of a credential, certificate, or degree.

Improving compensation

- Conduct a survey of staff salaries, compensation, and turnover.

- Establish a mechanism to collect such information on a regular basis.

- Hold focus groups to discuss possible salary scales.

- Advocate for the establishment of salary scales (tied to qualifications) when negotiating public contracts and increasing reimbursement rates.

- Provide assistance to programs attempting to improve salaries and benefits through pay equity and comparable worth (particularly in employer-supported programs such as colleges, hospitals, government agencies, and other large employers).

- Explore the possibility of linking early childhood staff with state or local health and retirement plans.

- Develop a salary enhancement fund (through legislation or a public/private partnership) that would provide additional money to all types of early childhood programs to increase salaries and benefits.

- Provide training to teacher-caregivers and family child care providers to speak out on their own behalf.

Increasing public awareness

- Develop a media release about the coalition.

- Hold a press conference to announce identified needs and strategies for action, once the needs are assessed and goals are developed.

- Submit articles or guest editorials to local newspapers about quality issues or discuss the issues on radio and television shows.

- Invite members of the press and public officials to coalition events.

- Hold hearings throughout the community or state (or ask the state legislature or city council to hold hearings) to discuss quality issues.

MORE POTENTIAL ACTIVITIES

Increasing public awareness, continued

- Develop a speakers group to make presentations about quality and to solicit support from the business community, civic associations, religious groups, parent groups, etc. Include parents as speakers.

- Develop a flyer or brochure suggesting what parents can do to help (or use existing NAEYC and CCEP brochures).

- Air programs about quality on the community public access television station.

Developing an affordability fund

- Enlist public and private support to establish an affordability fund of scholarships for parents to access high quality programs (accredited programs or certified providers) for their children.

- Use the establishment of such a fund to promote greater recognition of what constitutes quality.

Assessing progress

Throughout the life of a coalition, it is useful to periodically take stock of the group's accomplishments and the directions suggested by current activities. The following questions can be used to help develop an annual progress report or to help coalition members assess progress on an ongoing basis:

- How do current activities relate to the coalition's stated goals?
- What problems has the coalition faced?
- How have barriers been overcome?
- What has been accomplished?
- What strategies have worked best?
- Where should the coalition go from here?

TOGETHER TOWARD CHANGE: SUMMARY AND CONCLUSIONS

Despite differences, there is the potential sound of harmony.

The early childhood field is characterized by diversity. Providers work in different kinds of settings serving children of various ages; programs are run by different types of organizations with a variety of funding sources; various groups within the community are affected in different ways by a specific action; and the strategies to meet all these needs are numerous and diverse.

Despite these differences, there is the potential sound of harmony. All across the country, various groups are organizing to set higher standards, to expand training opportunities, to increase compensation, and to promote access to and recognition of quality early childhood services. Only through unified efforts can we avoid competition and strengthen our voice. Working together in coalitions at the state and local level, we can transcend our differences and join hands to reach our common goal of providing the very best services to young children and families.

NAEYC offers a variety of resources to support your Full Cost campaign

#537/The Full Cost of Quality: What You Should Know, What You Can Do companion brochure 50¢ each or 100 copies for $10

#765/3-inch round buttons declare "Children Are Worth It! Celluloid coated with a safety clasp. **25 for $12**

#766/1-1/4-inch round child's button says "My early childhood program is worth it!" Celluloid coated with a safety clasp. **25 for $8**

#768/14-inch round balloons-jumbo, deep blue and regal red balloons proclaim "Children are worth it!" **25 for $7**

#769/3-inch round stickers to distribute at conferences and other events. **500 for #25**

Other NAEYC resources of interest

Brochures
All brochures are 50¢ each or $10 for 100 copies of the same title.

#590/NAEYC Guiding Principles for the Development and Analysis of Early Childhood Legislation, NAEYC

#550/The Crisis is Real: Demographics on the Problems of Recruiting and Retaining Early Childhood Staff, Barbara A. Willer & Lynn C. Johnson

Books
#736/Quality, Compensation, and Affordability in Early Childhood Programs: An Action Kit **$10**

#224/Developmentally Appropriate Practice in Early Childhood Programs Serving Young Children Birth through Age 8, Sue Bredekamp, editor **$5**

#920/Accreditation Criteria and Procedures of the National Academy of Early Childhood Programs, Sue Bredekamp, editor **$6**

#140/Quality in Child Care: What Does Research Tell Us? Deborah Phillips, editor **$6**

#250/ A Great Place to Work: Improving Conditions for Staff in Young Children's Programs, Paula Jorde-Bloom **$5**

#270/Speaking Out: Early Childhood Advocacy, Stacie G. Goffin and Joan Lombardi **$6**

Reaching the Full Cost of Quality in early childhood programs will require collaborative efforts. Following is a selected list of organizations whose focus lends itself to involvement in this type of effort. Resources relevant to the Full Cost campaign are also listed.

Child Care Action Campaign
330 Seventh Avenue
New York, NY 10001
212-239-0138
Making Good Connections: Public-Private Partnerships in Child Care **$13** for CCAC members; **$23** for nonmembers

Child Care Employee Project
6536 Telegraph Avenue, Suite A-201
Oakland, CA 94609
415-653-9889
This organization is the only organization of its kind, dedicated solely to improving the status and working conditions of child care employees. In addition to the following resources, they offer technical assistance and resources for conducting salary surveys.

From the Floor: Raising Child Care Salaries **$10**

Raising Salaries: Strategies that Work **$5**

Critical Questions: What You Should Know about Your Child's Teachers (one-panel brochure) **$1 for 5 copies; $10 for 100 copies**

Who Cares? Child Care Teachers and the Quality of Child Care in America. Results of the National Child Care Staffing Study are presented in several formats, including
Executive summary **$10**

Final report **$25**

Local reports—individual reports of the findings for each of the five sites investigated—Atlanta, Boston, Detroit, Phoenix, and Seattle. **$5 per report**

Worthy Work, Worthless Wages **$2**

Children's Defense Fund
122 C Street, N.W.
Washington, DC 20001
Who Knows How Safe? The Status of State Efforts to Ensure Quality Child Care, Gina Adams **$5.95** (includes postage)

Ecumenical Child Care Network
National Council of Churches
475 Riverside Drive, Room 572
New York, NY 10115-0050
ECCN Policy Report #3: Caring for Ourselves: Wages and Benefits in Child Care **$4.50** for non-members

Exchange Press
P.O. Box 2890
Redmond, WA 98073
In addition to the bi-monthly publication, *Child Care Information Exchange*, Exchange Press offers a variety of resources targeted for early childhood program directors. Of particular note is *Caring Spaces, Learning Places*, Jim Greenman. **$29 + $2** shipping and handling

National Center for Clinical Infant Programs
2000 Fourteenth Street, North, Suite 380
Arlington, VA 22201-2500
703-528-4300
NCCIP's TASK (Training Approaches for Skills and Knowledge) project has produced four distinct but related documents:

Preparing practitioners to work with infants, toddlers, and their families:

Issues and recommendations for policymakers

Issues and recommendations for the professions

Issues and recommendations for educators and trainers

Issues and recommendations for parents

Each document is available for **$5 per copy**. All four documents may be purchased as a **set for $18**. Add **$2.25** for shipping and handling.

National Committee on Pay Equity
1201 16th Street, N.W.
Washington, DC 20036
202-822-7304
Bargaining for Pay Equity: A Strategy Manual, **$9 + $2** postage and handling

National Conference of State Legislatures
1560 Broadway, Suite 700
Denver, CO 80202
303-830-2200
The Child Care Guarantee in Welfare Reform, Lorraine A. Dixon-Jones, **$15**

National Association of Elementary School Principals
1615 Duke Street
Alexandria, VA 22314
703-684-3345
Early Childhood Education and the Elementary School Principal: Standards for Quality Programs for Young Children. **$14.95 + $2.50 postage and handling**

National Governor's Association
Center for Policy Research
444 N. Capitol Street, N.W.
Washington, DC 20001
Taking Care: State Developments in Child Care **$15 prepaid.** Send order, Attention: Publications.

National Head Start Association
1220 King Street, Suite 200
Alexandria, VA 22314
703-739-0875
Head Start Salaries, 1989-90 Staff Salary Survey, prepared by Raymond C. Collins **$10**

Other resources
Creative Benefits, *Association Digest*, 3,(3), Fall 1990, Greater Washington Society of Association Executives. This brief pamphlet includes several articles regarding the provision of employee benefits, including "Benefits with Muscle," "Keep 'em happy, health, and productive," "An apple a day," and "Providing for the family." **$4 per copy**
Contact: Suzanne Hajec, Production and Business Manager at GWSAE, 1426 21st Street, N.W., Suite 200, Washington, DC 20036-5901 202-429-9370

Who Cares for America's Children: Child Care Policy for the 1990s, Cheryl D. Hayes, John L. Palmer, and Martha J. Zaslow, editors
Available from National Academy Press, 2101 Constitution Avenue, N.W., Washington, DC 20418 **$24.95**

WORKSHEET #1: STAFFING WORKSHEET

GROUP NAME:	AM					NUMBER OF CHILDREN ENROLLED EACH HOUR									PM
	6:00	7:00	8:00	9:00	10:00	11:00	12:00	1:00	2:00	3:00	4:00	5:00	6:00	7:00
TOTAL NUMBER OF CHILDREN IN GROUP:	HOURS OF EACH STAFF MEMBER:														
AGE OF MAJORITY OF CHILDREN IN GROUP:	AM					NUMBER OF TEACHERS PRESENT EACH HOUR									PM

GROUP NAME:	AM					NUMBER OF CHILDREN ENROLLED EACH HOUR									PM
	6:00	7:00	8:00	9:00	10:00	11:00	12:00	1:00	2:00	3:00	4:00	5:00	6:00	7:00
TOTAL NUMBER OF CHILDREN IN GROUP:	HOURS OF EACH STAFF MEMBER:														
AGE OF MAJORITY OF CHILDREN IN GROUP:	AM					NUMBER OF TEACHERS PRESENT EACH HOUR									PM

GROUP NAME:	AM					NUMBER OF CHILDREN ENROLLED EACH HOUR									PM
	6:00	7:00	8:00	9:00	10:00	11:00	12:00	1:00	2:00	3:00	4:00	5:00	6:00	7:00
TOTAL NUMBER OF CHILDREN IN GROUP:	HOURS OF EACH STAFF MEMBER:														
AGE OF MAJORITY OF CHILDREN IN GROUP:	AM					NUMBER OF TEACHERS PRESENT EACH HOUR									PM

GROUP NAME:	AM					NUMBER OF CHILDREN ENROLLED EACH HOUR									PM
	6:00	7:00	8:00	9:00	10:00	11:00	12:00	1:00	2:00	3:00	4:00	5:00	6:00	7:00
TOTAL NUMBER OF CHILDREN IN GROUP:	HOURS OF EACH STAFF MEMBER:														
AGE OF MAJORITY OF CHILDREN IN GROUP:	AM					NUMBER OF TEACHERS PRESENT EACH HOUR									PM

GROUP NAME:	AM					NUMBER OF CHILDREN ENROLLED EACH HOUR									PM
	6:00	7:00	8:00	9:00	10:00	11:00	12:00	1:00	2:00	3:00	4:00	5:00	6:00	7:00
TOTAL NUMBER OF CHILDREN IN GROUP:	HOURS OF EACH STAFF MEMBER:														
AGE OF MAJORITY OF CHILDREN IN GROUP:	AM					NUMBER OF TEACHERS PRESENT EACH HOUR									PM

WORKSHEET #2: STAFF ROLES AND EDUCATIONAL QUALIFICATIONS

Directions: To complete worksheet, list all personnel fulfilling administrative, teaching, support and specialty roles and list relevant educational qualifications. Compare listed qualifications for those recommended for various positions on page 70. If an individual's degree is not in the field, but they have substantial coursework in the field, list qualifications under that degree.

Staff Role	Relevant Master's	Relevant Bachelor's	Relevant Associate's	CDA Credential	Some Training	No Training

WORKSHEET #3: COMPARING SALARIES FOR VARIOUS POSITIONS WITH COMPARABLE PROFESSIONALS WITHIN THE COMMUNITY

This worksheet should be used to compare staff positions requiring different levels of educational preparation and responsibility to comparable professionals within the community. Family child care providers should choose the position most comparable to their current levels of educational preparation and responsibility. This information may then be used to estimate a target salary level. Some programs may choose to identify a series of steps to reach the full cost target.

DIRECTOR				
Current Average Salary DIRECTOR	Public School Principal	Human Resources Manager	Health Services Administrator	TARGET

MASTER TEACHER				
Current Average Salary MASTER TEACHER	Public School Teacher*	Human Resources Specialist*	Registered Nurse*	TARGET

Base comparisons on individuals with comparable advanced preparation and higher levels of experience.

TEACHER				
Current Average Salary for TEACHER	**Public School Teacher***	**Human Resources Specialist***	**Registered Nurse***	**TARGET**

*Base comparisons on individuals with comparable preparation and levels of experience.

ASSISTANT TEACHER				
Current Average Salary for ASST. TEACHER	**Public School Asst. Teacher**	**Human Resources Assistant**	**Registered Nurse or Licensed Practical Nurse**	**TARGET**

*Base comparisons on individuals with comparable preparation and levels of experience.

TEACHING ASSISTANT				
Current Average Salary for TEACHING ASST.	**Public School Teacher Aide***	**Human Resources Office Assistant***	**Nurse's Aide***	**TARGET**

*Base comparisons on individuals with comparable preparation and levels of experience.

WORKSHEET #4: DETERMINING TOTAL COMPENSATION COSTS

Directions: To complete worksheet, list all personnel fulfilling administrative, teaching, support and specialty roles. General target salary is based on average comparable salary for the individual's role from Worksheet #3. Individual Target Salaries should be determined taking into account the individual's level of qualification and mastery of performance.

To estimate benefits: MULITIPLY Total Salaries by .20 or .25 to determine total benefits. depending on desired level (20% or 25%).

Staff member	Current Salary	General Target (from Wksht. #3)	Individual Target
Total Salaries			
Benefits			
TOTAL COMPENSATION			

WORKSHEET #5: BUDGET OF EARLY CHILDHOOD PROGRAM COSTS

BUDGET CATEGORY	CURRENT EXPENSES	ESTIMATED MARKET COSTS	SUBSIDY (Market less current costs)
PERSONNEL COSTS			
Director			
Other Educational/Support Specialists			
Teaching Staff			
Administrative Support Staff			
Other staff (cook, janitor, etc.)			
Substitutes/temporary labor			
TOTAL SALARIES			
BENEFITS			
PERSONNEL TAXES (FICA/Unemployment)			
TOTAL PERSONNEL COSTS			
OCCUPANCY COSTS			
Rent/Mortage			
Utilities			
Janitorial Service/Supplies			
Building/Grounds Maintenance			
TOTAL OCCUPANCY COSTS			
ADMINISTRATIVE COSTS			
Insurance (liability/property/theft/accident/etc.)			
Office Equipment (Copier/typewriter/computer and software/telephone and answering machine/etc.)			
Advertising			
Postage			
Licensing/Organizational Fees			
Taxes			
TOTAL ADMINISTRATIVE COSTS			

Budget, continued

BUDGET OF EARLY CHILDHOOD PROGRAM COSTS, CONTINUED

BUDGET CATEGORY	CURRENT EXPENSES	ESTIMATED MARKET COSTS	SUBSIDY (Market less current costs)
EDUCATIONAL PROGRAM COSTS			
Program supplies			
Program equipment			
Staff development			
Parent involvement			
Field trips			
Nutrition and food service			
Transportation			
Supplementary social services			
(Health/dental screening; vision/hearing screening; speech/language therapy; support services for serving children with special needs)			
Equipment/resources to support services for children with special needs			
TOTAL EDUCATIONAL PROGRAM COSTS			
TOTAL COSTS OF SERVICE PROVISION (add shaded areas)			

EQUITABLE FAMILY CHILD CARE BUDGET (ANNUAL EXPENSES)
Developed by Kathy Modigliani, Bank Street College

	TOTAL (Add shaded areas)
PERSONNEL *Equitable wages (estimate of wages that a person with similar education, experience, and reponsibilities would earn in other jobs in the community)* Provider Assistants and substitutes Other (e.g., Custodian*)	
TOTAL WAGES	
Benefits *@ 25% of Wages*	
TOTAL COMPENSATION **(Wages & Benefits)**	
FOOD	
Supplies and Equipment Toys and materials Office supplies, computer Household supplies* Equipment*	
TOTAL SUPPLIES AND EQUIPMENT	
Other Expenses Postage Copying Maintenance and repairs* Rent/Mortage, Utilities* Insurance Advertising Accountant Business entertaining/gifts Mileage/transportation Professional dues and publications Professional conference expenses	
TOTAL OTHER EXPENSES	
GRAND TOTAL	

Prorate the family child care portion of these expenses

To determine the Full Cost per child for full-time care, divide total expenses by the full-time equivalent number of children in the program. This is the full cost of full-time care that is not subsidized by the provider. **Kathy Modigliani** *is a member of the NAEYC Advisory Panel on Quality, Compensation, and Affordability.*

WORKSHEET #6: CHANGES NEEDED TO REACH FULL QUALITY		
PROGRAM CHARACTERISTICS: NEEDED IMPROVEMENTS	**OPTIONS FOR CHANGE**	**COST**
PROMOTING GOOD RELATIONSHIPS *Limited group size; good adult-child ratios; continuity in staffing*		
QUALIFIED STAFF WITH SPECIALIZED PREPARATION IN CHILD DEVELOPMENT/ EARLY EDUCATION *Staff appropriately prepared for level of responsibility; ongoing program for staff development*		

PROGRAM CHARACTERISTICS: STRENGTHS AND WEAKNESSES	OPTIONS FOR CHANGE	COST
ADEQUATE COMPENSATION *Staff compensation comparable to similar community professionals; good benefits package provided; career ladder in place*		
ESTABLISHING A GOOD ENVIRONMENT **FOR CHILDREN TO LEARN** *Safe, well-maintained facility with ample space and equipment; sufficient variety of developmentally appropriate learning materials and equipment provided through program budget* **FOR ADULTS TO WORK** *Staff lounge; personal storage areas; paid breaks; good working conditions; staff development and resource library available*		

WORKSHEET #7: FULL COST BUDGET FOR EARLY CHILDHOOD PROGRAMS

BUDGET CATEGORY	FULL COST
PERSONNEL COSTS	
Director	
Other Educational/Support Specialists	
Teaching Staff	
Administrative Support Staff	
Other staff (cook, janitor, etc.)	
Substitutes/temporary labor	
TOTAL SALARIES	
BENEFITS	
PERSONNEL TAXES (FICA/Unemployment)	
TOTAL PERSONNEL COSTS	
OCCUPANCY COSTS	
Rent/Mortage	
Utilities	
Janitorial Service/Supplies	
Building/Grounds Maintenance	
TOTAL OCCUPANCY COSTS	
ADMINISTRATIVE COSTS	
Insurance (liability/property/theft/accident/etc.)	
Office Equipment/Supplies	
Advertising	
Postage	
Licensing/Organizational Fees	
Taxes	
TOTAL ADMINISTRATIVE COSTS	
EDUCATIONAL PROGRAM COSTS	
Program Supplies/Equipment	
Staff Development	
Parent Involvement	
Field Trips	
Nutrition and Food Service	
Transportation	
Supplementary Social Services	
TOTAL EDUCATIONAL PROGRAM COSTS	
TOTAL COSTS OF SERVICE PROVISION	

INFORMATION ABOUT NAEYC

NAEYC is. . .

. . . a membership-supported organization of people committed to fostering the growth and development of children from birth through age 8. Membership is open to all who share a desire to serve and act on behalf of the needs and rights of young children.

NAEYC provides...

. . . educational services and resources to adults who work with and for young children, including

- *Young Children*, *the* journal for early childhood educators

- Books, posters, brochures, and videos to expand your knowledge and commitment to young children, with topics including infants, curriculum, research, discipline, teacher education, and parent involvement

- An **Annual Conference** that brings people from all over the country to share their expertise and advocate on behalf of children and families

- **Week of the Young Child** celebrations sponsored by NAEYC Affiliate Groups across the nation to call public attention to the needs and rights of young children and their families

- Insurance plans for individuals and programs

- Public affairs information for knowledgeable advocacy efforts at all levels of government and through the media

- **The National Academy of Early Childhood Programs**, a voluntary accreditation system for high-quality center-based programs for young children

- The **Information Service**, a centralized source of information sharing, distribution, and collaboration on a variety of topics affecting early childhood programs

For free information about membership, publications, or other NAEYC services, call NAEYC at 202-232-8777 or 800-424-2460 or write to NAEYC, 1834 Connecticut Avenue, N.W., Washington, DC 20009-5786.